In a Cuban Kitchen

ALEX GARCIA

In a Cuban Kitchen

RUNNING PRESS
PHILADELPHIA • LONDON

A QUINTET BOOK

9 8 7 6 5 4 3 2 1
Digit on the right indicates the number of this printing
Library of Congress Cataloging-in-Publication Number 2004090368

ISBN 0-7624-1541-X

This book was designed and produced by
Quintet Publishing Limited
6 Blundell Street
London N7 9BH

Co-written by Rebeka Four

Senior Project Editor: Corinne Masciocchi
Project Editor: Ruth Patrick
Editor: Erin Connell
Designer: Simon Daley
Photographer: Juliet Piddington
Food Stylist: Kathryn Hawkins
Creative Director: Richard Dewing
Publisher: Oliver Salzmann

This book may be ordered by mail from the publisher.
But try your bookstore first!

Running Press Book Publishers
125 South Twenty-second Street
Philadelphia, Pennsylvania 19103-4399
Visit us on the web!
www.runningpress.com

Manufactured in Singapore by Pica Digital Pte. Ltd.
Printed in China by SNP Leefung Printers Ltd.

Picture credits
Kevin R. Adlard: 5, 9, 10, 11, 19, 128
Getty Images: 7, 8, 12, 88, 101, 102, 116, 126, 166, 171

Contents

Introduction 6

Glossary 13

Tapas and snacks 15

Salads, sandwiches, and soups 31

Marinades, sauces, and dressings 59

Fish and seafood 69

Meat and poultry 93

Accompaniments and rice dishes 117

Desserts 139

Coffees and drinks 159

Index 175

Introduction

Left: Alex Garcia, age seven.

The years I have spent in kitchens—from my grandmother's to my parents', from my aunts' to my own—all seem to have been leading up to this very moment, when I can share the one true love and driving passion in my life—the homespun Cuban cooking from my childhood years. It is the inspiration for all that I am today as a chef, and most importantly, what makes me appreciate the endless pleasures that a simple, homemade meal offers to the palate, the senses, and the soul.

Growing up in Cuba, I was surrounded by the aromas, flavors, tastes, colors, and textures from the best of what Mother Nature has to offer. Cuba, fondly known as the jewel of the Caribbean, captivates visitors and natives alike with its beauty, bounty, and most notably, its warm and welcoming people. As a child in my grandmother's kitchen, and later in my mother's "sanctuary" (as she called her kitchen), my senses awoke as I embraced the soulful traditions of Cuban cooking. And it is here, in the kitchen—the heart of the Cuban home—where traditions and recipes are handed down from generation to generation. Cuban cooking is never just about preparing food; rather, it is a larger experience, born out of our culture and history. The warmth and comfort of Cuban food encourages diners to shed their inhibitions and invites them to partake in the joyful celebrations of life that are best shared with family and friends.

It was while sitting at my grandmother's table that I would learn of the births and breakups in the neighborhood, and find out who was dating Teresita, who lived two doors down! We all listened as our mothers and aunts told us that soaking the beans overnight was the secret to making the best *potaje* (creamy bean soup) on the block, or that if *el bistec de palomilla* (top round) was pounded and then marinated for at least three to four hours before cooking, you'd be guaranteed the juiciest steak you could wish for.

Cuban cooking is not tied to measurements, set cooking times, specific temperatures, or order and strict adherence to a list of ingredients. Rather, it is a chaotically precise display of what I like to call "artful intuition." A few key ingredients are essential for particular dishes, but other than these exceptions, everything else is highly flexible. For example, you would never substitute cilantro for culantro, but on

the other hand, a dash of Salsa de tomate Cubana (*see* page 64) or a vibrant *sofrito* will enhance almost any dish. And any Cuban knows that when in doubt, a pinch of cumin and a sprig of oregano will bring out the flavor in any recipe.

Cuban cooks do not like to follow recipes to the letter. Instead, we prefer to allow the ingredients to guide us as we develop each food's flavor to its fullest capacity. It is for this reason that I found it challenging to create the recipes for this book with the precision in measurement and direction that the home cook requires. So, I invite each one of you to try these recipes frequently, and with each attempt, work toward making them your very own. Feel out each dish. As you become familiar with the foods, your awareness of their intended tastes, textures, and aromas will become clearer, and you will feel more comfortable preparing the dishes with just a list of ingredients and a sense of the results you desire.

Cuban cuisine evolved out of the island's rich and varied history. Historians estimate that Cuba's first humans came from South America and are likely to have reached Cuba's shores around 3500 B.C. The Guanahatabey, who settled in the west, and the Siboney, who occupied much of the rest of the island, were fishermen and hunter-gatherers. The Tainos, who arrived from the east and were a part of the Arawak Indians, introduced agriculture, which led to the growing of *boniatos* (Cuban white sweet potatoes), *yuca* (cassava), yams, corn, pumpkins, peanuts, peppers, avocados, and tobacco.

On October 27, 1492, Christopher Columbus, or Cristóbal Colón as he is known in the Spanish-speaking world, sighted a large land mass, which would later come to be known as Cuba. He described it as "the most beautiful land human eyes have ever seen." Over the next 410 years, Cuba was controlled by many different nations. It was captured by the British in 1762, and then returned to Spain as trade for Florida, in 1763. Later controlled by the United States from 1898 to 1902, Cuba finally achieved its independence in 1902.

The Spanish people discovered many new ingredients throughout Cuba, and incorporated these foods into their own cuisine. Although they did not adopt the cooking styles of the indigenous inhabitants, the Spanish quickly exported these new foods to their homeland, adding greatly to the exchange of international food that was in the midst of developing. At the same time, the Spanish imported their own foods to Cuba, thus assimilated these products into the lives of the Cuban people.

In 1791, Haitian slaves organized to fight for independence, and French

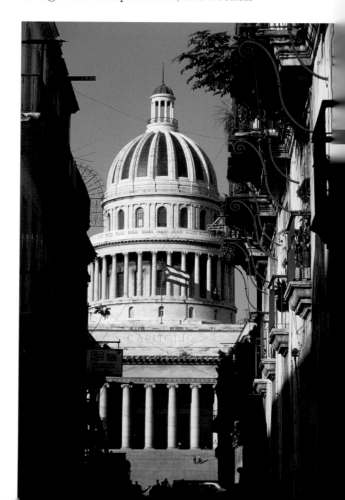

slave owners fled and took refuge in Cuba. These French immigrants brought with them new cooking methods which further enhanced the wealth of ingredients and techniques used in Cuba.

However, the most influential and lasting cultural contribution to Cuban culture and food comes from African slaves, who were brought to Cuba by the Spanish. They infused the Cuban way of life with an indelible, powerful, and magnificent depth and tradition. Africans introduced a new cooking method, and in doing so, gave birth to the Cuban stew. The slaves were forced to work long hours, and while they were out in the fields, they left stews at home to cook slowly over a fire. Often, this stew was the only meal the slaves ate all day long, so it had to be hearty and robust. The local Cuban people quickly adopted this way of cooking, and stews became a staple of Cuban cuisine. The *ajiaco* is undoubtedly the most popular Cuban stew, and appears in Cuban kitchens everywhere.

Today, Cuban cooking is an amalgamation of African, Spanish, European, and Arawak foods and cooking styles. As each conqueror brought new foods, flavors, and techniques to Cuba, the Cuban people added them to their ever-expanding cooking repertoire. Cuban cooking truly reflects the rich history of the island

and is a colorful and representative expression of Cuban life.

Food helps tell the story of the Cuban people. Our island has always welcomed weary travelers from far away lands, beckoning them to stay. Hospitality is an abundant resource, and is counted by the Cuban people as one of their most important treasures. Consequently, the diverse cultures that have become a part of the population have all contributed indelibly to Cuban cooking, making the food more energetic and flavorful.

A notable individual who took advantage of Cuba's hospitality was Ernest Hemingway. Regarded as one of Cuba's most prominent adopted sons, he fell in love with the island, its people, and its culture. Hemingway made Cuba his home for twenty years, and while living there, he wrote one of his best known works, *The Old Man and the Sea*.

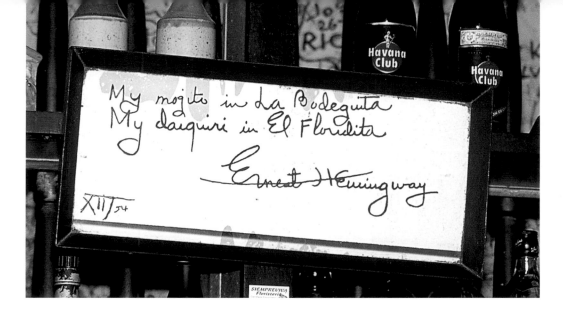

My mojito in La Bodeguita
My daiquiri in El Floridita

Ernest Hemingway

XII/54

Hemingway put the small, quaint restaurant La Bodeguita del Medio on the international map. This is where the mojito (*see* page 165), which is now served everywhere around the world, became Hemingway's elixir of choice. Rumor has it that he liked his mojito with a bit more rum than the recipe calls for. It is Hemingway's professed love for El Floridita, his favorite watering hole in Havana, that continues to attract throngs of visitors every year. This is the birthplace of the daiquiri (*see* page 164), a drink said to be especially concocted for Hemingway. There is even a daiquiri named for the famous author (*see* page 173).

The key to Cuban cooking is in the ingredients. Our cuisine is simple peasant food, and our "star chefs" are devoted mothers, grandmothers, aunts, and fathers, who cook simply using the enticing bounty around them.

Cuba is divided into provinces that fall within particular geographical regions, each of which possesses distinct soil characteristics. The province of Pinar del Río, located in the westernmost part of the island, is where our tobacco crops flourish. Just south of here, citrus thrives among countless acres of land on Isla de Pinos. Habana's farmlands produce viandas, or tubers, and vegetables.

Las Villas, the center of the island, is abundant with fruit, particularly *guayabas* (guavas). Further east is the province of Camaguey, where Cuba's cattle graze the vast, green pastures. Finally, there is Oriente, where coffee and sugarcane crops thrive.

Each season offers a different crop. Fruit begins to flower in the winter, during the months of December, January, and February. The *zafra*, or sugarcane harvest, happens during the winter months. The flowers finally come into bloom throughout the spring and early summer, during the months of March, April, May, and June. August brings with it avocados and their buttery flavor and rich color. Tubers, such as *boniato*, *yuca*, and *malanga* (taro), are plentiful all year long.

The revolution completely ended private ownership of any kind, including real estate. The government designated farming cooperatives to grow specific crops. The effect of thousands of acres of farmlands growing one single crop is hypnotic and enthralls the senses. Endless territories are covered with plants such as guavas, which permeate the air with their aroma for hundreds of miles. In Isla de Pinos, where citrus is grown, countless fields seem to burst with golden

oranges, bright yellow lemons, and vibrant green limes.

While I was growing up in Cuba, my father worked as an engineer for the National Institute for Agrarian Reform. I spent my summers away from school traveling with my dad through the deepest countryside and remotest Cuban farmlands. All year long, I would eagerly await the end of school, not so much because I did not enjoy it, but because having to attend got in the way of my adventures and journeys with my father and his crew.

My dad and his team of experts would survey farms around Havana to determine the irrigation method that would produce the best crops possible. All day long, we would feast on fruits and vegetables plucked right from the vines and branches on which they grew, or pulled from the earth that nourished them. I, of course refused to heed my dad's warnings, and always managed to overindulge my senses, ending up with a bellyache from eating too much.

I believe that every Cuban who leaves the island and chooses to make his or her home elsewhere secretly yearns to return home one day. This yearning is why I have especially selected each of the recipes in the pages to follow. For no matter where I find myself in the world, each time I cook one of these dishes, I come as close as possible to reliving my childhood in Cuba.

Every meal I cook, and every ingredient I select and prepare unearths a vivid snapshot of an unforgettable moment from my youth.

In the Cuba I left behind, everyone in the neighborhood contributed to a meal. Each yard offered trees and homegrown vegetable and herb gardens, where no one needed to ask permission to pluck lemons from the tree or take some culantro and parsley from the garden. There was an unspoken understanding that your neighbor's bounty was communal property. In fact, everyone on my block knew that they should help themselves to my grandmother's still warm, freshly laid chicken's eggs if they wanted to make the best scrambled eggs possible. Hardships made mealtimes a group effort. Every neighbor's resources were offered and shared in earnest. A little borrowing and bartering yielded remarkable results. This ardent collaboration gave way to the birth of the *paladares*.

Cuba is filled with paladares in every city and in the countryside. A paladar is simply someone's home where anyone can go for a delicious, homemade meal. You know by word of mouth which homes are paladares. As you enter, you go straight to the kitchen and help yourself to whatever is on the stove, before pulling up a chair in the dining room table. On the way out, you pay the cook a nominal fee for what is sure to have been unforgettable food, prepared with the freshest ingredients available.

A Cuban kitchen located anywhere in the world is always ready to feed more than just those who reside within the home. Any Cuban cook you meet will tell you that the first, second, and third rules of Cuban cooking are "donde come uno comen dos y donde comen dos comen todos," which means, "where one eats, two eat, and where two eat, all eat."

It is my sincere desire that the recipes I share with you here awaken an awareness of each ingredient's texture, flavor, and aroma. Please explore and tantalize your palate with the wondrous bounties nature generously bestows upon us. ¡*Buen apetito!*

Glossary

Ancho chile a broad, dried chile ranging in flavor from mild to pungent. The rich, slightly fruit-flavored ancho is the sweetest of the dried chiles.

Banana leaves used to wrap foods for steaming.

Bijol a yellow coloring used in cooking, similar to turmeric. It is used in rice, soup, chicken, meat, and fish dishes.

Boniato a Cuban sweet potato with white flesh rather than the yellow or orange flesh of other varieties. Irregular in shape, the skin color can vary from reddish to cream colored. It is drier and not as sweet as other varieties of sweet potato.

Bonito tuna a small tuna rarely exceeding 25 pounds. It ranges from moderate to high fat and is the most strongly flavored of the tunas.

Calabaza also called the West Indian pumpkin. This round, pumpkin-like squash can range in size from as large as a watermelon to as small as a cantaloupe. It has a sweet flavor similar to that of butternut squash and its texture is firm and succulent.

Canilla rice long grain white rice.

Chayote a fruit the size and shape of a very large pear. The flesh, which surrounds one soft seed, is white and rather bland-tasting. It is widely available during winter months, but can be found in some food stores throughout the year.

Chorizo sausage a highly seasoned, coarsely ground pork sausage flavored with garlic, chili powder, and other spices. The casing should be removed and the sausage crumbled before cooking.

Crème de cacao and dark crème de cacao a dark, chocolate-flavored liqueur with a hint of vanilla. Dark crème de cacao is a darker form of the same liqueur.

Cubanelle pepper also known as Italian frying pepper, the Cubanelle pepper is large and blocky. It is light green in appearance and it matures red. Its thin walls make it an excellent choice for frying. This pepper is not hot.

Culantro not to be confused with cilantro. It is a flavorful herb used in Caribbean cooking. It is a tastier substitute for cilantro.

Guava paste or candied guayaba purée a popular dessert throughout Latin America. The paste or purée is made from guayabas or guavas. These are tropical fruit that have a mildly sweet pink pulp and a green to yellow exterior, depending on ripeness.

Habana Club a Cuban rum. Aged three years it is silver/white in color; aged five years it is gold/dark; and añejo is aged for seven years.

Malanga closely related to the taro root. It is about the size and shape of a regular white potato with the outer skin brown and somewhat hairy.

Malbec a rich French red wine grape grown in Bordeaux.

Maraschino liqueur a bittersweet, cherry-flavored Italian liqueur made from wild marasca cherries and their crushed pits.

Pequillo pepper a Hungarian fire-roasted red pepper from Spain.

Pimento a large, red, heart-shaped sweet pepper. Its flesh is sweet, succulent, and more aromatic than that of the red bell pepper.

Plantain a large, firm variety of banana extremely popular in Latin American countries. Also referred to as a "cooking banana." It has a mild, almost squash-like flavor and is used very much as a potato would be in the United States.

Red curaçao an orange-flavored liqueur made from the dried peel of bitter oranges.

Ruby port considered the lowest grade of port. It is blended from several vintages and is the lightest and fruitiest of ports.

Salt cod salted and dried cod.

Salt-cured beef beef that has been dried and packed in salt preparations.

Serrano ham a Spanish ham similar to the Italian Parma ham.

Sofrito a sauce made by sautéing annatto seeds in rendered pork fat. The seeds are removed before chopped onions, green bell peppers, garlic, pork, and various herbs are cooked in the flavored oil until the ingredients are tender and the mixture thick. The sauce is used in recipes as needed.

Tardio wine a sweet wine made from Torrontes grapes picked late in the Argentine harvest season. It is floral in aroma, and rich in honey, grapefruit, apricot, and peach flavors.

Tocino fatback; the fresh unsmoked and unsalted layer of fat that runs along the pig's back.

Triple Sec a strong, clear orange-flavored liqueur very similar to curaçao.

Yerba buena similar to spearmint. The leaves have a milder flavor and fragance than its cousin, peppermint.

Yuca also called cassava or manioc. It is a root that ranges from 6 to 12 inches in length and has a tough brown skin which, when peeled, reveals a crisp, white flesh. There are two main categories: sweet and bitter, and the latter is poisonous unless cooked.

Tapas and snacks

Tres croquetas

*No Cuban party is ever without this staple dish, which is a true
Cuban favorite. This recipe comes straight from my grandmother's
handwritten recipe book. She uses it as a base and varies it by changing
the meat she uses, because you can never serve just one flavor of
croquetas at a time. (I personally prefer to leave the nutmeg out of
the fish version.) And she has definitely mastered their traditional
"finger shape." Unlike her, I just shape mine into small balls.*

Croquetas de jamón

HAM CROQUETTES

Makes 6 to 8 • Cooking time: 20 minutes

Olive oil, for frying

3 pounds smoked ham, chopped

1 medium white onion, chopped

2 medium red bell peppers, chopped

2 garlic cloves, sliced

2 tablespoons tomato paste

¼ bunch fresh parsley, chopped

½ teaspoon fresh grated nutmeg

½ cup heavy cream

1 cup all-purpose flour

Salt and fresh ground black pepper, to season

2 eggs, lightly beaten

2 cups cracker meal

Canola oil, for frying

1 Heat the olive oil in a large skillet and cook the ham, onion, bell peppers, and garlic for about 8 minutes. Stir in the tomato paste and cook until it caramelizes. Add the parsley, nutmeg, and heavy cream. Sprinkle in ½ cup of the flour and season with salt and pepper. Let the mixture cool for a while until about room temperature.

2 Put the mixture through a meat grinder, using a number two setting. Shape the mixture into finger-shaped sticks, or small patties.

3 Bread these croquetas by first dipping them into the remaining flour, then the eggs, and finally into the cracker meal.

4 Pour 1 inch of canola oil into a skillet and heat to 375° F on a frying thermometer. Fry the croquetas until golden brown.

Top: Croquetas de pollo; *Center:* Croquetas de mariscos;
Bottom: Croquetas de jamón

Croquetas de pollo

CHICKEN CROQUETTES

Makes 6 to 8 • Cooking time: 25 minutes

Olive oil, for frying

3 pounds boneless chicken breast and thighs, chopped

1 medium white onion, chopped

2 medium red bell peppers, chopped

2 garlic cloves, sliced

2 tablespoons tomato paste

¼ bunch fresh parsley, chopped

½ teaspoon fresh grated nutmeg

½ cup heavy cream

1 cup all-purpose flour

Salt and fresh ground black pepper, to season

2 eggs, lightly beaten

2 cups cracker meal

Canola oil, for frying

1 Heat the olive oil in a large skillet and cook the chicken, onion, peppers, and garlic for about 8 minutes or until the chicken is fully cooked. Stir in the tomato paste and cook until it caramelizes. Add the parsley, nutmeg, and heavy cream. Sprinkle with ½ cup of the flour, and season with salt and pepper. Let the mixture cool for a while until about room temperature.

2 Put the mixture through a meat grinder using a number 2 setting. Shape the mixture into finger-shaped sticks, or small patties.

3 Bread these croquetas by first dipping them into the remaining flour, then the eggs, and finally into the cracker meal.

4 Pour 1 inch of canola oil into a skillet and heat to 375° F on a frying thermometer. Fry the croquetas until golden brown.

Croquetas de mariscos

SEAFOOD CROQUETTES

Makes 6 to 8 • Cooking time: 20 minutes

Olive oil, for frying
1 pound white fish fillets, chopped
1 pound shrimp, cleaned, shelled,
  and deveined
1 pound lump crabmeat,
  picked clean
1 medium white onion, chopped
2 medium red bell peppers,
  chopped
2 garlic cloves, sliced

2 tablespoons tomato paste
¼ bunch fresh parsley, chopped
½ teaspoon fresh grated nutmeg
½ cup heavy cream
1 cup all-purpose flour
Salt and fresh ground black
  pepper, to season
2 eggs, lightly beaten
2 cups cracker meal
Canola oil, for frying

1 Heat the olive oil in a large skillet and cook the fish, shrimp, crabmeat, onion, bell peppers, and garlic for about 8 minutes or until all the fish is fully cooked. Stir in the tomato paste and cook until it caramelizes. Add the parsley, nutmeg, and heavy cream. Sprinkle with ½ cup of the flour, and season with salt and pepper. Let the mixture cool for a while until about room temperature.

2 Put the mixture through a meat grinder using a number 2 setting. Shape the mixture into finger-shaped sticks, or small patties.

3 Bread these croquetas by first dipping them into the remaining flour, then the eggs, and finally into the cracker meal.

4 Pour 1 inch of canola oil into a skillet and heat to 375° F on a frying thermometer. Fry the croquetas until golden brown.

Tostones con Picadillo de Cayo Hueso

FRIED GREEN PLANTAINS TOPPED WITH PICADILLO

Serves 6 • Cooking time: 1 hour

1 pound top choice ground beef

1 teaspoon dried oregano

1 teaspoon ground cumin

¼ cup olive oil

2 garlic cloves, chopped fine

1 medium white onion,
  chopped fine

1 small green bell pepper,
  chopped fine

½ cup dry white wine

1 cup tomato sauce

Salt and fresh ground black
  pepper, to season

Vegetable oil, for frying

4 large green plantains, peeled and
  cut into diagonal 1½-inch rounds

1 medium chopped tomato,
  to garnish

1 Thoroughly combine the beef, oregano, and cumin in a mixing bowl.

2 Heat the oil in a skillet and cook the garlic, onion, and bell pepper until soft. Add the meat mixture, wine, and tomato sauce. Cover the pan and cook over a medium to low heat for 15 minutes. Then remove the lid and cook, uncovered, for a further 15 minutes, or until the liquid is fully reduced, making sure that the meat is still moist. Season with salt and pepper and set aside.

3 Pour 1 inch of vegetable oil into a skillet. Heat the oil until it reaches 375° F on a frying thermometer. Fry the plantains for about 8 minutes, being sure to turn them several times until they are soft all the way through. Set the oil aside and transfer the plantains to a dish. Place a wet towel over them, and pressing down with your hands, smash the plantains until they are completely flattened out into thin disks.

4 Reheat the oil to very high temperature. Fry the smashed plantains again until crispy on both sides. Serve the ground beef in small bowls garnished with the chopped tomato. Scoop up the meat with the plantain tostones.

Mariquitas

CRISPY FRIED PLANTAIN SLICES

Serves 4 • Cooking time: 10 minutes

Vegetable oil, for frying
4 green plantains, peeled and cut
   lengthwise into very thin slices
Salt, to season

Heat the oil in a skillet until it reaches 350° F on a frying thermometer.
Fry the plantains until crispy. Transfer them to paper towels to drain.
Season with salt and serve immediately.

Bocaditos de bonito

BITE-SIZED TUNA SANDWICH SNACK

Serves 4 • Preparation time: 10 minutes

6 ounces oil-packed tuna

1 small red onion, chopped
   very fine

1 celery stalk, chopped very fine

1 medium roasted red bell pepper,
   chopped very fine

1 tablespoon mayonnaise

Salt and fresh ground black
   pepper, to season

12 slices white bread

1 cucumber, cut lengthwise into
   thin slices

Celery leaves, to garnish

1 Drain the tuna and place in a mixing bowl. Add the onion, celery, roasted pepper, and mayonnaise, and mix well. Season with salt and pepper.

2 Place 6 pieces of bread on a flat surface. Place 6 slices of cucumber on each piece of bread, laying them side by side. Be sure to stay within the crust when placing the cucumber slices. Scoop equal amounts of the tuna on top of the layer of cucumber. Top with 6 more slices of cucumber.

3 Close the sandwiches by topping with the remaining bread and cut the crusts off each sandwich, using the edges of the cucumber as a guide. Then cut each sandwich into 4 pieces. Garnish with celery leaves.

Enchilado de cazón

BABY SHARK CREOLE STYLE

Serves 4 • Cooking time: 30 minutes

½ cup olive oil

1 large white onion, sliced fine

2 medium Cubanelle or Italian
 frying peppers, sliced fine

2 medium roasted red bell peppers,
 sliced fine

2 garlic cloves, chopped

1 bay leaf

½ cup dry white wine

1 teaspoon white vinegar

3 tablespoons tomato paste

2 pounds cazón (baby shark
 fillets), diced

Salt and fresh ground black
 pepper, to season

1 teaspoon hot red pepper sauce

¼ bunch parsley, stems removed
 and leaves chopped

¼ bunch cilantro, stems removed
 and leaves chopped

1 Heat the oil in a medium skillet and fry the onion, Cubanelle peppers, roasted peppers, and garlic until soft, for about 5 minutes.

2 Add the bay leaf, wine, and vinegar and bring to a boil. Stir in the tomato paste. Add the cazón and cook, covered, for about 10 minutes. Season with salt and pepper. Add the hot sauce, parsley, and cilantro and serve hot.

Frituras de maíz

CORN FRITTERS

Serves 4 • Cooking time: 15 minutes

2 cups corn kernels, fresh if
  available
2 tablespoons all-purpose flour
½ teaspoon salt
3 medium eggs

1 tablespoon melted butter
½ cup sugar (optional)
Vegetable oil, for frying
Parsley, to garnish

1 Purée the corn kernels in a food processor or blender. Transfer to a mixing bowl and add the flour and salt.

2 Beat in the eggs one at a time. Add the melted butter and mix to completely combine. If you prefer sweet fritters, add the sugar at this time.

3 Heat the oil to about 350° F on a frying thermometer. Using a spoon to shape the fritters, drop them into the oil and fry until crispy and brown. Serve hot and garnish with parsley.

Cocktail tropical

FRESH SHRIMP WITH TROPICAL COCKTAIL SAUCE

Serves 6 • Cooking time: 10 minutes

1 medium tomato, halved

1 small white onion, halved

1 quart water, salted

1 lemon, halved

1 medium white onion, halved

1 generous pound (about 40 to 50)
   peeled small shrimp, cut in
   half lengthwise

Ice water

½ cup lime juice

½ cup orange juice

½ cup ketchup

1 to 2 tablespoons vinegary
   Mexican hot sauce (such as
   Temecula, Valentina, or Bufalo)

2 tablespoons olive oil

2 small ripe avocados, peeled,
   pitted, and cubed

2 medium tomatoes, chopped fine

1 small red onion, chopped fine

⅓ cup chopped fresh cilantro,
   plus several sprigs to garnish

Salt, to season

Tostadas, tortilla chips, or saltine
   crackers, to serve

1 Broil the halved tomato and small white onion and set aside.

2 Combine the salted water, lemon halves, and medium white onion halves in a large stockpot and bring to a boil. Add the shrimp and cook for 3 minutes. Remove the shrimp from the pan and transfer to a bowl of ice water.

3 Purée the broiled tomato, broiled onion, lime juice, and orange juice in a food processor. Transfer the mixture to a mixing bowl and add the ketchup, hot sauce, and olive oil, and mix. Add the shrimp, avocados, tomatoes, red onion, and cilantro. Season with salt and chill for about 1 hour.

4 Spoon the mixture into sundae glasses, Martini glasses, or small bowls. Garnish with sprigs of cilantro and serve with tostadas, tortilla chips, or saltines.

Fritura de ostiones

CUBAN-STYLE FRIED OYSTERS

Serves 4 • Cooking time: 5 minutes

1 medium egg

4 tablespoons water

1 cup cracker meal

1 teaspoon paprika

1 teaspoon fresh ground
  black pepper

1 teaspoon dried oregano

1 teaspoon dried thyme

16 oysters, shucked and well
  drained

Vegetable oil, for frying

Salsa de aguacate
  (*see* page 62), to serve

1 Whisk the egg and water in a medium bowl to thoroughly combine.

2 Combine the cracker meal, paprika, black pepper, oregano, and thyme in a food processor. Process briefly to a medium to fine consistency. Transfer to a dish and set aside.

3 Dip the oysters, one at a time, first into the egg and then into the seasoned cracker meal mixture. Shake to remove any excess breading.

4 Place 1 inch of oil in a large skillet and heat until the oil reaches 350° F on a frying thermometer. Drop the oysters into the hot oil and cook until golden brown on all sides, for about 1 minute. Remove the oysters with a slotted spoon and transfer to paper towels to drain. Serve the oysters on the cleaned half shells topped with Salsa de aguacate.

Entremes de camarones

SHRIMP TAPAS

Serves 4 • Cooking time: 20 minutes

8 sweet plantains (yellow but
   not overripe), peeled and
   cut into 3 pieces
2 tablespoons olive oil
1 small white onion, chopped fine
1 small green bell pepper,
   chopped fine

1½ pounds shrimp, cleaned, shelled,
   deveined, and chopped
Salt and fresh ground black
   pepper, to season
Vegetable oil, for frying

1 Place the plantains in a saucepan and cover with water. Bring to a boil and cook until tender, for about 15 minutes. Remove from the heat and drain. While the plantains are still hot, mash them and set aside.

2 Heat the oil in a skillet. Cook the onion, bell pepper, and shrimp for about 3 minutes. Season with salt and pepper. Transfer the shrimp mixture to the plantains and mix thoroughly to combine.

3 Scoop a large tablespoon of the plantain and shrimp mixture and, using your hands, form the mixture into a 1½-inch ball. Repeat until all the mixture has been used.

4 Pour about 2 inches of oil into a large skillet and heat until the oil reaches 375° F on a frying thermometer. Fry the balls until they are golden brown. Transfer to paper towels to drain. Serve hot.

Salads, sandwiches, and soups

Ensalada real

HEARTS OF PALM SALAD

Serves 4

2 medium vine-ripe tomatoes
1 cup olive oil
Salt, to season

One 10-ounce can hearts of palm,
 drained and sliced diagonally
4 scallions, sliced fine
1 medium red onion, sliced fine

1 To make the dressing, cut the tomatoes into quarters, remove the pulp, and set aside. Place the pulp in a blender. With the blender running at high speed, add the oil in a steady stream. Season with salt and set aside.

2 Combine the tomato quarters, hearts of palm, scallions, and red onion in a mixing bowl and drizzle with the dressing.

Croqueta preparada

CROQUETTE SANDWICH

Serves 4 • Cooking time: 8 minutes

Four 8-inch long pieces of Cuban
 bread or French baguette
8 cooked Croquetas de jamón
 (*see* page 17)
8 ounces ham, sliced fine

4 ounces Swiss cheese, sliced fine
3 pickles, sliced fine lengthwise
4 tablespoons yellow deli mustard
6 ounces butter

1 Slice the pieces of bread in half. Layer a croquette, some ham, and some cheese on one half of the bread. Top with pickle slices.

2 Spread 1 tablespoon of mustard on the other half of the bread and place on top of the sandwich to close. Spread the outside of the sandwich with butter and heat in a hot cast iron skillet, or on an electric griddle.

Ensalada de bacalao

SALT COD SALAD

Serves 4 • Cooking time: 25 minutes

1 pound salt cod
1 medium white onion, diced
6 jumbo green olives, pitted
and sliced

5 tablespoons olive oil
2 tablespoons red wine vinegar
Fresh parsley and lemon wedges,
to garnish

1 Cover the fish with water and soak in a medium saucepan for 2 hours, changing the water after the first hour.

2 Drain the fish. Return to the saucepan with fresh water and bring to a boil, then simmer for 20 minutes. Remove the pan from the heat, drain the fish, and leave until cool enough to handle.

3 Flake the fish, being sure to discard all the skin and dark meat. Combine the flaked fish with the onion, olives, olive oil, and vinegar in a mixing bowl. Serve chilled, garnished with parsley and lemon wedges.

Mariscada

SEAFOOD SOUP

Serves 6 • Cooking time: 2½ hours

Olive oil, for cooking

2 medium white onions, chopped

2 medium green bell peppers, chopped

Two 1½-pound lobsters, heads removed and reserved, tail still in its shell sliced into 1-inch thick pieces, and claws cracked

8 ounces large shrimp, peeled, cleaned, and deveined, shells reserved

1 cup canned tomato sauce

1 cup white wine

2 bay leaves

4 cups clam juice

4 cups water

24 Little Neck clams, cleaned

24 mussels, cleaned

Pinch saffron

8 ounces sea scallops, cleaned

½ bunch culantro, chopped fine

Salt and fresh ground black pepper, to season

1 Add enough olive oil to thinly coat the bottom of a large saucepan. Cook one of the onions and one of the bell peppers until soft.

2 Add the lobster heads and shrimp shells and cook until the shells begin to turn red. Next add the tomato sauce, white wine, and 1 of the bay leaves. Add the clam juice and water and cook for at least 2 hours. Strain and reserve the seafood broth.

3 Coat the bottom of a medium saucepan with olive oil and cook the other onion and bell pepper until the onion is soft.

4 Add the clams, mussels, the other bay leaf, and a pinch of saffron. Pour in the reserved seafood broth and simmer, uncovered, for about 20 minutes.

5 Add the shrimp, scallops, and lobster and cook for about 8 minutes. Finally add the culantro and season with salt and pepper.

Ensalada de mariscos

SEAFOOD SALAD

Serves 4 • Cooking time: 20 minutes

2 lemons, cut in half

2 bay leaves

½ teaspoon hot red pepper sauce

Salt, to season

8 ounces shrimp, peeled, cleaned,
   and deveined

Ice water

4 ounces scallops

3 medium calamari (squid),
   cut into rings

Olive oil, for frying

2 cloves garlic, sliced

24 Little Neck clams, cleaned

¼ cup white wine, or more if needed

24 mussels, cleaned

¼ bunch thyme, stems removed
   and chopped fine

1 small red onion, chopped fine

1 stalk of celery, chopped fine

1 roasted red pepper, chopped fine

4 fresh basil leaves, chopped fine

1 tablespoon olive oil

½ teaspoon fresh lime juice

Basil leaves, to garnish

1 Fill a large stockpot three-quarters of the way full with water and bring to a boil. Add the lemons, bay leaves, hot sauce, and salt. Cook for a few minutes, then add the shrimp and cook for about 4 minutes.

2 Remove the shrimp, leaving the cooking water in the pot, and immediately transfer the shrimp to a bowl of ice water. Bring the cooking water back to a boil and repeat the process with the scallops, cooking for 3 minutes, and then the calamari, cooking for 1 minute. Add more ice to the water as necessary.

3 Coat the bottom of a skillet with olive oil and cook the garlic until it is golden. Add the clams and wine, adding more wine if needed. Cover and steam for 4 minutes, or until the first clams begin to open. Add the mussels, and cook until both the clams and mussels open.

4 Remove the clams and mussels from the pan and set aside, leaving the pan on the heat. Add the thyme to the pan and reduce the broth by three-quarters. Strain and let cool until about room temperature.

5 Combine the onion, celery, roasted pepper, basil, 1 tablespoon olive oil, and lime juice in a bowl. Cut the shrimp and scallops in half and add to the bowl, along with the strained broth. Remove the mussels and clams from the shells and add to the mix. Check for seasoning, adding salt and pepper as needed. Let marinate in the refrigerator for at least 30 minutes before serving, garnished with basil leaves.

Media noche

HAM, ROASTED PORK, AND SWISS CHEESE ON SWEET BREAD

Serves 8 • Cooking time: 8 minutes

4 sweet rolls, sliced in half

8 ounces roasted pork shoulder
or leg, sliced fine

8 ounces ham, sliced fine

4 ounces Swiss cheese, sliced fine

2 dill pickles, sliced fine lengthwise

4 tablespoons yellow deli mustard

6 ounces butter

1 To assemble each sandwich, layer some roasted pork, some ham, and some cheese on one half of a roll. Top with some dill pickle slices.

2 Spread 1 tablespoon of the mustard on the inside of the other half of the roll and place the top of the roll over the sandwich to close.

3 Spread the top and bottom of the outside of the sandwich with butter and cook in a very hot cast-iron skillet, or on an electric griddle, until heated through and golden brown on the outside.

Yucassoise

COLD YUCA SOUP

Serves 6 • Cooking time: 1½ hours

2 to 3 small whole fresh yucas, peeled, or 1 pound frozen yuca

Water, salted

3 tablespoons salted butter

2 cloves garlic, chopped fine

2 medium leeks, white parts only, cleaned well and chopped fine

4 cups chicken broth

2 cups milk

Salt and fresh ground black pepper, to season

Chopped chives, to garnish

1 Place the yucas in a medium saucepan and cover with salted water. Simmer over a medium heat until tender, for about 35 minutes. Remove the yuca from the heat, drain, and set aside.

2 Melt the butter in a small skillet over a low heat. Add the garlic and leeks and cook until soft, for about 12 minutes. Meanwhile, cut the yuca into small pieces, removing the stringy core. Add the yuca to a food processor and purée. Return the purée to the saucepan and add the garlic-leek mixture.

3 Gradually add the broth and milk and cook over a low heat, whisking vigorously, until the soup is smooth and well blended. Remove from the heat and season with salt and pepper. Let the soup cool to room temperature and then refrigerate for several hours until thoroughly chilled. If you prefer a thinner soup, add more milk and check for seasoning. Serve in chilled bowls sprinkled with chopped chives.

Sopa de frijoles colorados

RED BEAN SOUP

Serves 4 • Cooking time: about 2 hours

8 cups water

1 pound dried red beans, sorted
and rinsed

1 medium Cubanelle pepper,
cut in half, seeds removed

2 bay leaves

2 tablespoons olive oil

4 ounces bacon, diced

4 ounces ham, diced

4 ounces Spanish chorizo
sausage, diced

1 red, green, and yellow bell
pepper, chopped fine

1 large white onion, chopped fine

2 garlic cloves, chopped fine

¼ cup tomato paste

1 large potato, peeled and diced

8 ounces calabaza (West Indian
pumpkin), peeled and diced

Salt, to season

½ bunch culantro, chopped fine

1 Put the water, beans, Cubanelle pepper, and bay leaves in a large stockpot and bring to a boil over a medium to high heat. Reduce the heat to low and partially cover the pot. Cook, stirring occasionally, until the beans are tender, for about 1½ hours. Remove from the heat and discard the Cubanelle pepper pieces and bay leaves. Set aside.

2 Heat the olive oil in a skillet over a medium heat and cook the bacon, ham, and chorizo for about 4 minutes. Add the bell peppers, onion, and garlic and cook until the onion is soft. Stir in the tomato paste.

3 Return the beans to the heat and add the cooked pepper mixture and potato. Simmer for 15 minutes.

4 Add the calabaza and cook for a further 10 minutes or until the calabaza and potato are tender. Season with salt and simmer gently for 5 minutes to blend the flavors. Add the culantro before serving.

Front: Sopa de frijoles colorados; *Back:* Sopa de frijoles negros

Sopa de frijoles negros

BLACK BEAN SOUP

Serves 4 • Cooking time: 2 hours

8 cups water

1 pound dried black beans,
  sorted and rinsed

1 medium Cubanelle or Italian
  frying pepper, quartered
  lengthwise

2 bay leaves

2 tablespoons, plus ½ cup olive oil

1 red, green, and yellow bell pepper,
  chopped fine

1 large white onion, chopped fine

¼ cup tomato paste

½ tablespoon ground cumin

½ tablespoon dried oregano

5 garlic cloves, chopped fine

1 tablespoon sugar

1 tablespoon white vinegar

Salt, to season

Fresh oregano, to garnish

1 Put the water, black beans, Cubanelle pepper, and bay leaves in a large saucepan and bring to a boil over a medium to high heat. Reduce the heat to low and partially cover the pan. Cook, stirring occasionally, until the beans are tender, for about 1½ hours.

2 Remove the pan from the heat and discard the pepper and bay leaves. Set aside.

3 Heat the 2 tablespoons olive oil in a skillet and cook the bell peppers and onion over a medium heat until soft. Stir in the tomato paste and add the cumin and oregano. Cook for about 5 minutes and set aside.

4 In a separate skillet, cook the garlic in the remaining olive oil over a medium to low heat until golden. Return the beans to the heat and add the pepper mixture, garlic in its oil, the sugar, and vinegar. Season with salt and simmer gently for 20 minutes to blend the flavors. Garnish with a sprig of fresh oregano.

Guiso de quimbobo

OKRA STEW

Serves 4 • Cooking time: 2 hours

1 pound okra, washed and
　cut into ¼-inch slices
1 cup water
2 teaspoons white vinegar
1 teaspoon lemon juice
4 ounces bacon, diced
2 tablespoons olive oil
1 medium white onion,
　chopped fine
1 medium green bell pepper,
　chopped fine

2 tomatoes, chopped fine
2 garlic cloves, chopped fine
½ pound pork, cut into ½-inch cubes
½ cup Salsa de tomate Cubana
　(*see* page 64), or canned
　tomato sauce
2 quarts chicken broth
2 sweet plantains, diced
Salt and fresh ground
　black pepper, to season

1 Soak the okra in the water,
vinegar, and lemon juice for
15 minutes to eliminate the slime.

2 Add the bacon and oil to a
medium saucepan and cook to
render the bacon fat. Add the onion,
bell pepper, tomatoes and garlic
and cook for about 4 minutes, or
until translucent. Add the pork
and cook for a further 5 minutes.
Add the tomato sauce or salsa and
cook for 10 minutes.

3 Add the okra and chicken broth,
and bring to a boil. Finally add
the plantains and cook for about
20 minutes. Season with salt and
pepper.

Ensalada de coditos

CUBAN-STYLE PASTA SALAD

Serves 4 • Cooking time: 8 minutes

Water, for cooking
8 ounces elbow macaroni
2 hard-cooked eggs, diced
1 cup mayonnaise
2 tablespoons Dijon mustard
1 cup frozen sweet peas, thawed

One 6-ounce can pimentos,
chopped fine
8 kalamata (black) olives,
pitted and sliced
Salt and fresh ground black
pepper, to season

1 Bring water to a boil in a medium saucepan. Add the macaroni and cook for about 8 minutes. Drain and let cool.

2 Place the macaroni in a mixing bowl and add the eggs, mayonnaise, and mustard, and mix thoroughly. Add the peas, pimentos, and olives and mix to combine. Season with salt and pepper.

Chicharos requetecubanos

CUBAN-STYLE SPLIT PEA SOUP

Serves 6 • Cooking time: 1 1/2 hours, plus overnight soaking

1 pound dried split peas, rinsed, sorted, and soaked overnight
2 1/2 quarts water
2 bay leaves
12 ounces smoked ham, sliced fine
1/4 cup olive oil
4 ounces bacon, chopped fine

2 cloves garlic, chopped fine
1 medium white onion, chopped fine
1 teaspoon ground cumin
2 teaspoons dried oregano
Salt and fresh ground black pepper, to season

1 Drain the peas and discard the soaking water. Put the water, peas, bay leaves, and ham in a large saucepan and bring to a boil over a medium heat. Reduce the heat to low and simmer, covered, until tender, for about 45 minutes, adding more water if necessary. Set aside.

2 Make a sofrito by heating the oil in a skillet and cooking the bacon, garlic, and onion for about 4 minutes. Add the cumin and oregano and cook until fragrant, for a further 2 minutes.

3 Add the sofrito to the peas and cook for about 15 minutes. Season with salt and pepper

Sandwich Cubano

CUBAN SANDWICH

Serves 4 • Cooking time: 8 minutes

**Four 8-inch long pieces of Cuban
  bread or French baguette**
**8 ounces roasted pork shoulder
  or leg, sliced fine**
8 ounces ham, sliced fine

4 ounces Swiss cheese, sliced fine
2 dill pickles, sliced fine lengthwise
4 tablespoons yellow deli mustard
6 ounces butter

1 Slice the pieces of bread in half. To assemble each sandwich, layer some roasted pork, some ham, and some cheese on one half of the bread. Top with some dill pickle slices.

2 Spread 1 tablespoon of the mustard on the inside of the top half of the bread and place it over the sandwich to close. Spread the top and bottom of the outside of the sandwich with butter and cook in a very hot cast-iron skillet, or on an electric griddle, until heated through and golden brown on the outside.

Choripan

CHORIZO SANDWICH

Serves 4 • Cooking time: 10 minutes

1 small white onion, sliced fine
Olive oil, for cooking
**Four 8-inch long pieces of Cuban
  bread or French baguette**
8 smoked Spanish chorizo

**sausages, cut into ¼-inch
  thick slices**
2 dill pickles, sliced lengthwise
4 tablespoons yellow deli mustard
6 ounces butter

1 Fry the onion in the oil until translucent. Slice the bread lengthwise. Divide the chorizo, fried onions, and dill pickles into four equal portions.

Above: Choripan

2 Assemble the sandwiches by placing chorizo on top of one half of the bread and top with onions. Place the sliced dill pickle on top. Spread the inside of the other slice of bread with mustard and close the sandwich.

3 Spread the top and bottom of the outside of the sandwich with butter and cook in a very hot cast-iron skillet, or on an electric griddle, until heated through and golden brown on the outside.

Judías

WHITE BEAN SOUP

Serves 6 • Cooking time: 2 hours plus overnight soaking

1 pound dried white beans, rinsed,
   sorted, and soaked overnight

2½ quarts water

2 bay leaves

One 6-ounce piece salt pork

2 medium ham hocks (lower
   portion of the hind leg)

¼ cup olive oil

2 cloves garlic, chopped fine

1 medium white onion, chopped
   fine

1 teaspoon ground cumin

2 teaspoons dried oregano

Salt and fresh ground black
   pepper, to season

1 Drain the beans and discard the soaking water. Place the beans, water, bay leaves, salt pork, and ham hocks in a large saucepan and bring to a boil over a medium heat. Reduce the heat to low and simmer, covered, until tender, for about 1½ hours, adding more water if necessary.

2 Remove the salt pork from the saucepan and discard. Remove the ham hocks and shred the meat, discarding the fat. Add the shredded meat to the beans and set aside.

3 Make a sofrito by heating the oil in a skillet and cooking the garlic and onion for about 3 to 4 minutes. Add the cumin and oregano and cook until fragrant, for a further 2 minutes. Add the sofrito to the beans and cook for about 15 minutes. Season with salt and pepper.

Ensalada de chayote y aguacate

CHAYOTE AND AVOCADO SALAD

Serves 4 • Cooking time: 8 minutes

Water, for cooking

4 chayotes, peeled, seeded, and cut into large cubes

1 medium avocado, peeled, pitted, and diced

6 tablespoons extra virgin olive oil

3 tablespoons white vinegar

¼ bunch fresh cilantro, chopped fine

½ teaspoon sugar

½ teaspoon Dijon mustard

Salt and fresh ground black pepper, to season

1 Bring the water to a boil in a medium saucepan and add the chayote. Cook until tender for about 4 to 5 minutes Remove the pan from the heat, drain the chayote, and let cool.

2 Place the chayote in a bowl and add the avocado. In a separate bowl, combine the oil, vinegar, cilantro, and sugar. Stir in the mustard and mix well. Season with salt and pepper Add the dressing to the chayote and avocado, mix, and serve.

Guiso de maíz

CORN STEW

Serves 8 • Cooking time: 1 hour

2 tablespoons olive oil

4 ounces bacon, chopped fine

2 Spanish chorizo sausages,
chopped fine

1 medium white onion,
chopped fine

1 medium red bell pepper,
chopped fine

2 cloves garlic, chopped fine

1 cup canned whole tomatoes,
drained and chopped

3 tablespoons sherry

8 cups chicken broth

1 medium potato, peeled and diced

1 cup calabaza (West Indian
pumpkin), peeled and diced

8 large ears corn, kernels removed
(about 4 cups)

Salt and fresh ground black
pepper, to season

¼ bunch culantro, chopped,
to garnish

1 Heat the oil in a large saucepan until fragrant, then add the bacon
and cook until crisp. Reduce the heat to low and add the chorizo, onion,
red bell pepper, and garlic. Cook, stirring, until the vegetables are
tender, for about 6 to 8 minutes.

2 Add the tomatoes, sherry, chicken broth, potato, and calabaza. Cook,
covered, for a further 20 minutes. Then add the corn and season with
salt and pepper. Cook, partially covered, until all the vegetables are
tender, for a further 20 minutes.

3 Check the seasoning, adding more salt and pepper if necessary.
Garnish with the culantro and serve in warmed bowls.

Sopa de pollo de la abuela

GRANDMOTHER'S CHICKEN SOUP

Serves 6 • Cooking time: 1 hour

1 whole fryer chicken, cleaned,
  washed, and skin removed,
  cut into 8 pieces
1 large malanga (taro root), peeled
  and cut into medium cubes
1 cup calabaza (West Indian
  pumpkin), diced
1 large yuca, peeled and diced
1 green plantain, peeled and cut
  into 1-inch slices
2 quarts chicken broth
½ teaspoon dried oregano

½ teaspoon ground cumin
4 whole garlic cloves, peeled
6 whole black peppercorns
1 large green bell pepper, seeded
  and quartered
1 large white onion, chopped
Salt, to season
2 garlic cloves, chopped fine
1 medium red bell pepper, cut into
  8 pieces
4 culantro leaves

1 Place the chicken, malanga, calabaza, yuca, plantain, and chicken broth in a very large stockpot and bring to a low boil.

2 Add the oregano, cumin, whole garlic cloves, peppercorns, green bell pepper, and onion. Cook, covered, for about 30 minutes, skimming the excess fat from the surface.

3 Remove the green bell pepper and season with salt. Add the garlic and red bell pepper and cook for a further 10 minutes. Check the seasoning and adjust to taste.

4 Add the culantro and cook, uncovered, over a very low heat, for a further 10 minutes.

Ensalada criolla

CREOLE SALAD

Serves 4

1 large avocado, peeled, pitted,
   and cut into chunks
2 medium tomatoes, diced
1 medium red onion, diced

6 tablespoons **Vinagreta Cubana**
   (*see* page 60)
Salt, to season

Place the avocado, tomatoes, and onion in a mixing bowl. Add the
vinaigrette and mix to combine. Season with salt.

Cocido Habanero

CABBAGE, SPANISH SAUSAGE, AND CHICKPEA SOUP

Serves 4 • Cooking time: 3 hours plus overnight soaking for chickpeas

8 ounces dried chickpeas, soaked

2½ quarts water

1 bay leaf

Two 8-ounce smoked ham hocks
  (lower portion of the hind leg)

4 Spanish chorizo sausages

8-ounce slab bacon, chopped

2 potatoes, peeled and quartered

2 carrots, cut into 1½-inch slices

¼ cup olive oil

1 large white onion, quartered

1 large red bell pepper, quartered

1 garlic clove, chopped fine

¼ cup tomato paste

½ white cabbage, chopped

Fresh bread, to serve

1 Drain the chickpeas and discard the soaking water. Place the chickpeas, water, bay leaf, and ham hocks in a large saucepan. Bring to a simmer and cook for 2 hours.

2 Add the chorizo, bacon, potatoes, and carrots, and cook for a further 30 minutes, or until the potatoes are tender. Reduce the heat and continue cooking, adding more water if necessary.

3 Heat the oil in a skillet and cook the onion, bell pepper, and garlic until soft. Stir in the tomato paste and cook for a further 2 minutes.

4 Add the pepper mixture and cabbage to the saucepan and cook for 20 minutes, or until the chickpeas are soft and the soup has thickened. Serve with fresh bread.

Pan con lechón

PORK SANDWICH

Serves 4 • Cooking time: 3½ hours

One 4- to 6-pound pork shoulder,
  deboned
4 whole garlic cloves, peeled
1 medium white onion, diced large
1 bay leaf
1 teaspoon fresh oregano
1 teaspoon ground cumin
1½ cups white vinegar
½ bunch fresh cilantro,
  leaves picked from the stems

Salt and fresh ground black
  pepper, to season
2 cups lard
Olive oil, for frying
2 small red onions, sliced fine
Juice of 2 limes
Four 8-inch long pieces Cuban
  bread or French baguette
1 tablespoon butter

1 With a sharp knife, make a few incisions in the pork shoulder and stud with the garlic cloves, inserting them in the surface of the meat.

2 Purée the onion, bay leaf, oregano, cumin, white vinegar, and cilantro in a blender and season with salt and pepper. Pour this marinade over the pork and refrigerate for at least 2 hours.

3 Preheat the oven to 325° F. Remove the pork from the marinade and place in a roasting pan.

4 Heat the lard until it is melted and pour over the pork. Cover the pork with aluminum foil and bake for 3 hours. Remove the pork from the oven and let rest at least 15 minutes before cutting into thin slices.

5 In a skillet, cook the red onions in some olive oil until soft and deglaze the pan with the lime juice.

6 To assemble each sandwich, layer 4 to 5 slices of pork on one half of the bread. Pour some of the onion mixture on top and close the sandwich by placing the other half of bread on top. Spread butter on the outside of the bread. On a hot cast-iron skillet, or electric griddle, heat the sandwich until the bread is crispy on both sides.

Frita Cubana

CUBAN HAMBURGER

Serves 4 • Cooking time: 30 minutes

1 pound ground beef
1 pound ground pork
½ white onion, grated
2 garlic cloves, crushed
2 tablespoons paprika
½ teaspoon ground cumin
1 teaspoon dried oregano
2 teaspoons salt
Vegetable oil, for frying

2 potatoes, peeled and sliced fine
4 Kaiser or white bread rolls,
    cut in half
2 medium tomatoes,
    cut into 8 slices
1 small red onion, cut into
    8 thin slices
French fries for serving
4 tablespoons yellow deli mustard

1 In a mixing bowl, thoroughly mix the beef, pork, onion, garlic, paprika, cumin, oregano, and salt. Divide the meat equally to make 4 patties, and refrigerate for 1 hour.

2 Heat 1 inch of oil in a skillet. Fry the potatoes until crispy. Set aside.

3 In the same skillet, pan-fry the patties, turning once, until cooked through, for about 4 minutes per side.

4 To assemble each hamburger, place a patty on the bottom half of a roll and top with a tomato slice, an onion slice, and serve with French fries. Spread 1 tablespoon of mustard on the inside of the top half of the roll and place over the patty to close.

Marinades, sauces, and dressings

Marinado de batidora

Makes 3½ cups

½ bunch fresh parsley

½ bunch fresh cilantro

½ bunch fresh oregano

3 bay leaves

6 whole garlic cloves, peeled

1 medium white onion, quartered

1 medium red onion, quartered

6 whole black peppercorns

1 cup white vinegar

3 cups olive oil

Salt, to season

Place the parsley, cilantro, oregano, bay leaves, garlic, white and red onions, peppercorns, and vinegar in a heavy-duty blender or food processor and blend thoroughly. Transfer the mixture to a mixing bowl and add the oil. Season with salt.

This marinade is used to marinate pork, beef, or chicken.

Vinagreta Cubana

CUBAN VINAIGRETTE

Makes 1½ cups

2 tablespoons yellow deli mustard

1 large garlic clove, crushed

6 tablespoons fresh lime juice or
   white vinegar

¾ cup extra virgin olive oil

¼ bunch fresh parsley, stems

removed and leaves chopped

¼ bunch fresh cilantro, stems
   removed and leaves chopped

Salt and fresh ground black pepper,
   to season

Combine the mustard, garlic, and lime juice in a mixing bowl. Whisk in the oil in a steady stream. Add the parsley, cilantro, salt, and pepper and mix thoroughly. Use to dress salads.

Opposite: Vinagreta Cubana

Marinado Cubano basico

BASIC CUBAN MARINADE

Makes 1 cup

3 garlic cloves, chopped
Juice of 3 limes
½ cup olive oil
¼ bunch fresh parsley, stems removed and leaves chopped

¼ bunch fresh cilantro, stems removed and leaves chopped
Salt, to season

Combine all the ingredients in a mixing bowl and season with salt. Use to marinate meats and poultry overnight.

Salsa de aguacate

AVOCADO DRESSING

Serves 4

1 large ripe avocado, peeled, pitted, and chopped
1 teaspoon white vinegar
3 teaspoons olive oil

1 tablespoon fresh lime juice
Water
Salt and fresh ground black pepper, to season

Add the avocado, vinegar, olive oil, and lime juice to a blender and purée, adding water as needed. Season with salt and pepper and use to flavor any vegetable salad or with any seafood dish. You can also make it a little thicker and serve it as a dip.

Opposite: Salsa de aguacate

Salsa Criolla

CREOLE SAUCE

Serves 4 • Cooking time: 15 minutes

½ cup extra virgin olive oil
3 cloves garlic, chopped
½ bay leaf
2 large white onions, chopped fine
2 medium green bell peppers,
   chopped fine

5 medium tomatoes, chopped fine
½ teaspoon pimentón (paprika)
Salt and fresh ground black pepper,
   to season

1 Heat the olive oil in a skillet. Add the garlic, bay leaf, onions, bell peppers, and tomatoes, and cook over a medium heat, stirring until thickened. Add the pimentón and remove from the heat.

2 Season with salt and pepper and serve hot or cold with meat and poultry dishes.

Salsa de tomate Cubana

CUBAN-STYLE TOMATO SAUCE

Serves 8 • Cooking time: 1 hour

½ cup olive oil
1 large white onion, diced
3 medium Cubanelle or Italian
   frying peppers, diced
5 garlic cloves, chopped
3 tablespoons tomato paste

Three 10-ounce cans whole
   tomatoes, mashed with a fork
5 fresh basil leaves
1 teaspoon sugar
Salt and fresh ground black
   pepper, to season

1 Heat the olive oil in a large saucepan over a medium heat. Add the onion, peppers, and garlic and cook until soft. Stir in the tomato paste and cook for about 5 minutes.

Above: Salsa Criolla

2 Add the tomatoes and simmer for about 45 minutes. Then add the basil and sugar. Season to taste with salt and pepper. Remove from the heat and let cool slightly. Purée in a blender or food processor.

This sauce is used as a dipping sauce, to flavor stews, or to serve with pasta.

Sofrito

SOFRITO SAUCE

Makes 4 cups • Cooking time: 15 minutes

½ cup extra virgin olive oil

3 cloves garlic, chopped

½ bay leaf

2 large white onions, chopped fine

2 medium green bell peppers, chopped fine

5 medium tomatoes, chopped fine

3 tablespoons tomato paste

½ cup dry white wine

½ teaspoon pimentón (paprika)

¼ bunch fresh parsley, stems removed and leaves chopped fine

¼ bunch fresh cilantro, stems removed and leaves chopped fine

¼ bunch fresh oregano, stems removed and leaves chopped fine

Salt and fresh ground black pepper, to season

1 Heat the oil in skillet. Add the garlic, bay leaf, onions, bell peppers, and tomatoes, and cook over a medium heat until the onions are soft.

2 Stir in the tomato paste and let caramelize. Add the white wine and cook for 3 minutes then add the pimentón, parsley, cilantro, and oregano.

3 Remove from the heat and let cool slightly. Purée and season with salt and pepper.

This sauce is used to flavor stews, soups, and beans, and to thicken and flavor other sauces.

Marinado de naranja agria

BITTER ORANGE MARINADE

Makes 1 cup

3 garlic cloves, chopped fine

Juice of 3 bitter oranges,
    or 2 oranges and 1 lime

3 tablespoons olive oil

¼ bunch fresh oregano, stems
    removed and leaves chopped fine

1 bay leaf, chopped fine

¼ teaspoon ground cumin

Salt, to season

Combine all the ingredients in a mixing bowl and season with salt.

This marinade is used to marinate or cook pork.

Mojo criollo para viandas y carnes

HOT GARLIC SAUCE

Serves 4 • Cooking time: 10 minutes

¼ cup olive oil

1 medium white onion, chopped fine

6 garlic cloves, chopped

½ bunch fresh parsley, stems removed and chopped fine

½ bunch fresh cilantro, stems removed and chopped fine

Juice of 3 limes

½ teaspoon salt

1 Heat the olive oil in a medium saucepan. Add the onion and garlic and cook until fragrant.

2 Remove from the heat and let sit for 2 minutes. Add the parsley, cilantro, lime juice, and salt. Serve hot over vegetables or meat dishes.

Fish and seafood

Salpicón de pescado

Serves 4 to 6 • Cooking time: 1 hour

1 quart water

1 cup white wine

1 bay leaf

6 peppercorns

1 lemon, cut in half

1 large white onion, cut in half

1 carrot, cut in half

1 teaspoon hot red pepper sauce

3 pounds cod fish fillets

1 cup fine bread crumbs

2 tablespoons milk

2 tablespoons all-purpose flour

2 tablespoons olive oil

3 medium eggs, beaten

1 cup roasted red bell pepper, chopped fine

1 large dill pickle, chopped very fine

1 large white onion, diced

1 teaspoon dried oregano

Salt, to season

Large piece cheesecloth

3 hard-cooked eggs

Mixed salad, to serve

Lemon wedges, to garnish

1 Combine the water, wine, bay leaf, peppercorns, lemon, onion halves, carrot, and hot sauce in a large stockpot and bring to a boil. Continue boiling for 5 minutes to release the flavors. Strain and reserve the liquor, discarding the ingredients.

2 Return the cooking liquor to the pot and bring to a very slow simmer over a low heat. Add the fish fillets and cook for 4 minutes. Remove the fish and let cool to room temperature, again reserving the cooking water.

3 Flake the fish by hand and place in a mixing bowl. Add the bread crumbs, milk, flour, and olive oil. Add the beaten eggs, roasted pepper, pickle, diced onion, and oregano and mix well. Season with salt.

4 Fold the cheesecloth into an 18 x 18-inch piece, making it two layers thick. Scoop the fish mixture onto the edge of the cloth that is closest to your body and form a sausage-like shape about 10 inches long.

5 Place the hard-cooked eggs next to each other in the middle of the

sausage, pressing into the mixture until the eggs are firmly set. Fold each end of the cloth over the sausage. Taking the edge of the cloth closest to your body, roll the mixture along the width of the cloth, leaving a 1-inch space at the end. Cut off the excess cloth and use it to securely tie into a sausage shape. Put the sausage back into the pot with the reserved cooking liquid.

6 Cook over a medium heat for 45 minutes, making sure to keep the water at a low simmer. Remove from the pot and remove the cheesecloth while the sausage is hot; otherwise, the cloth will stick. Let the sausage cool to room temperature and then cut into ¾-inch slices. Serve cold with a mixed salad and garnish with lemon wedges.

Pudín de pescado

FISH CASSEROLE

Serves 6 to 8 • Cooking time: 1 hour 40 minutes

1 pound baking potatoes, peeled
   and diced
Two 1-pound white fish fillets
   (preferably cod), cleaned and
   skin removed
2 medium white onions, 1 cut in
   half, the other diced
1 lemon, cut in half
3 bay leaves
1 tablespoon olive oil
3 slices white bread

1 cup milk
5 medium eggs, beaten
½ teaspoon salt
¼ bunch fresh parsley, stems
   removed and leaves chopped fine
3 tablespoons butter, or
   cooking spray
Arroz amarillo (*see* page 126),
   to serve
Ensalada de chayote y aguacate
   (*see* page 49), to serve

1 Preheat the oven to 350° F. Place the potatoes in a medium saucepan. Cover with water and bring to a boil, cooking for about 15 minutes. Remove from the heat and drain. Purée the potatoes and set aside.

2 Place the fish fillets, onion halves, lemon halves, and 1 bay leaf in a medium saucepan. Cover with water and bring to a boil, cooking for about 8 minutes. Remove from the heat and drain. Using your hands, break the fish into flakes. Set aside.

3 Heat the olive oil in a skillet. Cook the remaining bay leaves and the diced onion until the onion is soft, for about 5 minutes. Remove from the heat, discard the bay leaves, and set aside.

4 In a food processor, process the bread to make coarse crumbs. Mix the bread crumbs, milk and beaten eggs in a large mixing bowl. Add the potato purée, fish, onion, salt, and parsley and mix to thoroughly combine.

5 Grease a 9-inch baking pan with butter or cooking spray. Pour the fish mixture into the pan and bake for about 1 hour. Serve with Arroz amarillo and Ensalada de chayote y aguacate.

Calamares rellenos

STUFFED SQUID

Serves 4 • Cooking time: 1½ hours

12 ounces ground veal

12 ounces ground pork

1 teaspoon dried oregano

1 teaspoon ground cumin

½ cup olive oil

3 whole garlic cloves, peeled

2 medium white onions, chopped
  fine, divided

1 small green bell pepper,
  chopped fine

1 cup dry white wine

1 cup tomato sauce

8 green olives, pitted and sliced

¼ cup raisins

Salt and fresh ground black
  pepper, to season

12 extra-large calamari (squid)
  tubes, cleaned

Toothpicks

1½ Cubanelle or Italian frying
  peppers, chopped fine

2 garlic cloves, chopped fine

One 10-ounce can whole tomatoes,
  crushed by hand

1 bay leaf

Salad, to serve

Fresh parsley, to garnish

1 Thoroughly combine the veal, pork, oregano, and cumin in a mixing bowl.

2 Heat ¼ cup of the olive oil in a skillet and, over a medium heat, cook the 3 whole garlic cloves, 1 of the onions, and the bell pepper until soft, for about 4 minutes.

3 Add the meat mixture, ½ cup of the wine, and the tomato sauce. Cover and cook over a medium to low heat for about 15 minutes.

4 Uncover the pan, mix in the olives and raisins, and cook for a further 15 minutes, or until the liquid is almost fully reduced, making sure that the meat is still moist. Season with salt and pepper. Remove from the heat and let cool.

5 Stuff the calamari with the meat mixture and close the ends with toothpicks. Set aside. Preheat the oven to 325° F.

6 Heat the remaining olive oil in a medium saucepan over a medium heat and cook the remaining onion, Cubanelle peppers, and garlic until soft, for about 4 minutes.

7 Add the tomatoes and the bay leaf, and bring the mixture to a boil. Immediately remove from the heat and pour into a 9-inch rectangular baking pan.

8 Arrange the stuffed calamari in the pan and cover with aluminum foil. Bake in the oven for 45 minutes or until the calamari are tender. Serve with a side salad and garnish with parsley.

Bacalao a la Viscaina

SALT COD, VISCAYA STYLE

Serves 6 • Cooking time: 45 minutes plus overnight soaking

1 pound salt cod, skin removed
   and deboned
1 pound baking potatoes, peeled
   and sliced
4 teaspoons olive oil
1 medium white onion,
   chopped fine
2 garlic cloves, chopped fine
1 green bell pepper, chopped fine
1 teaspoon white vinegar
One 6-ounce can pimentos,

drained and chopped fine
½ cup white wine
½ cup **Salsa de tomate Cubana**
   (*see* page 64), or prepared tomato
   sauce
6 large green olives,
   pitted and sliced
Sliced, toasted bread or French
   baguette, to serve

1 Rinse the cod and soak overnight prior to cooking, being sure to change the water three to four times. Rinse the cod thoroughly just before cooking.

2 Place the fish in a medium saucepan. Cover with water and bring to a boil, cooking for 10 minutes. Remove from the heat and drain. Using your hands, break the fish into flakes, being sure the fish is completely clean. Set aside.

3 Meanwhile, place the potatoes in a medium saucepan. Cover with water and bring to a boil, cooking for 15 minutes. Remove from the heat, drain, and set aside.

4 Heat the olive oil in a medium skillet. Add the onion, garlic, bell pepper, vinegar, and pimentos, and cook for 5 minutes. Add the white wine, Salsa de tomate Cubana, and fish. Cook for about 15 minutes, stirring well. Add the potatoes and olives and cook for a further 5 minutes. Remove from the heat and serve with toasted bread or French baguette.

Cherna a la Valenciana

GROUPER, VALENCIA-STYLE

Serves 4 • Cooking time: 15 minutes

3 pounds grouper fillets
Salt and fresh ground black
  pepper, to season
¼ cup all-purpose flour
Olive oil, for cooking

4 whole cloves garlic, peeled
1½ cups fish broth
Pinch saffron
¼ bunch fresh parsley, stems
  removed and leaves chopped

1 Season the fish fillets with salt and pepper. Dip the fish into the flour to coat both sides, reserving the remaining flour. Set the fish aside.

2 Coat the bottom of a skillet with ¼-inch olive oil and heat over a medium heat until fragrant. Add the garlic and cook until golden. Remove the garlic from the oil, chop, and set aside.

3 Add the fish to the pan and cook it, for about 45 seconds each side, until browned. Set aside.

4 Sprinkle the remaining flour into the oil. Lightly stir until the flour becomes paste-like in consistency. Slowly add half the broth, stir, then add the remaining broth, stirring thoroughly. Add the reserved garlic, saffron, and parsley, and stir well.

5 Return the fish to the pan and cook for about 8 minutes. If the sauce becomes too thick, add more broth as needed.

Pargo relleno

WHOLE RED SNAPPER STUFFED WITH SEAFOOD

Serves 4 • Cooking time: 25 minutes

2 tablespoons olive oil

1 small white onion, chopped fine

1 medium red bell pepper, chopped fine

2 medium tomatoes, chopped fine

1 clove garlic, chopped fine

1 cup dry white wine

1 chipotle pepper, chopped fine

8 ounces shrimp, peeled, cleaned, deveined, and chopped fine

8 ounces cooked lobster meat, chopped fine

8 ounces lump crabmeat, picked clean

¼ bunch fresh parsley, stems removed and leaves chopped fine

Salt and fresh ground black pepper, to season

4 whole red snappers

3 scallions, diced

8 ounces butter, cut up into 1-inch pieces

Lime wedges, chopped scallions, and fresh parsley, to garnish

1 Preheat the oven to 375° F. Heat the olive oil in a skillet over a medium heat and fry the onion, red bell pepper, tomatoes, and garlic until soft.

2 Add ½ cup of the wine and the chipotle pepper, and cook until the liquor is almost evaporated. Add the shrimp and cook for 1 minute.

3 Stir in the lobster, crabmeat, parsley, salt, and pepper. Remove from the heat.

4 With a sharp knife slit open each red snapper along its side so that it opens flat but do not cut all the way through. Carefully debone and clean the fish. Spoon a quarter of the seafood mixture into each snapper and close, securing with toothpicks. Place the four stuffed snapper into a baking dish. Pour in the remaining wine and add the scallions and butter. Bake for 25 minutes. Serve, garnished with lime wedges, scallions, and parsley.

Camarones rebozados

EGG-BATTERED SHRIMPS

Serves 4 • Cooking time: 10 minutes

4 medium eggs, beaten
Salt and fresh ground black
   pepper, to season
18 extra-large shrimp, cleaned,
   peeled, deveined, and sliced
   lengthwise to flatten

2 cups all-purpose flour
Olive oil, for cooking
2 cups Salsa de tomate Cubana
   (*see* page 64)
¼ bunch cilantro, stems removed
   and leaves chopped fine

1 Season the eggs with salt and pepper.

2 Dip the shrimp into the flour, then the eggs, and then the flour again.

3 Pour some oil into a skillet and heat until it reaches 350° F on a frying thermometer. Cook the shrimp for 30 seconds per side. Add the Salsa de tomate Cubana and cook for a further 3 minutes. Add the cilantro. Ideal served with fresh white rice and lemon wedges.

Raya alcaparrada

SKATE WITH CAPER SAUCE

Serves 4 • Cooking time: 20 minutes

1 cup all-purpose flour

Salt and fresh ground black
   pepper, to season

3 pounds skate, cleaned and
   deboned

Olive oil, for frying

1 large white onion, cut into
   thin strips

2 garlic cloves, chopped fine

1 medium Cubanelle or Italian
   frying pepper, sliced fine

One 6-ounce can tomato paste

1 tablespoon white vinegar

½ cup dry white wine

½ teaspoon ground cumin

½ teaspoon dried oregano

16 green olives, pitted and sliced

¼ cup raisins

¼ cup capers

1 Mix the flour with salt and pepper. Lightly coat the fish with the flour. Heat the olive oil in a skillet and over a high heat quickly cook the fish for two minutes on each side. Remove the fish from the skillet and set aside.

2 Using the same pan, cook the onion, garlic, and Cubanelle pepper until they are soft, for about 4 minutes. Add the tomato paste, vinegar, and wine, and bring to a boil. Add the cumin and oregano and cook for 5 minutes. Add the olives, raisins, and capers and cook for a further 2 minutes. Put the fish back in the pan, cover, and cook for 4 minutes.

Enchilado de camarones

CREOLE-STYLE SHRIMP

Serves 4 • Cooking time: 20 minutes

½ cup olive oil

1 large white onion, diced

2 medium **Cubanelle or Italian frying peppers**, diced

2 roasted red bell peppers, diced

2 garlic cloves, chopped

1 bay leaf

½ cup dry white wine

1 teaspoon white vinegar

3 tablespoons tomato paste

2 pounds shrimp, peeled, cleaned, and deveined

Salt and fresh ground black pepper, to season

1 teaspoon hot red pepper sauce

¼ bunch fresh parsley, stems removed and leaves chopped

¼ bunch fresh cilantro, stems removed and leaves chopped

1 Heat the olive oil in a medium saucepan. Over a medium heat, cook the onion, Cubanelle pepper, roasted pepper, and garlic until soft, for about 5 minutes. Add the bay leaf, wine, and vinegar. Bring to a boil and stir in the tomato paste.

2 Add the shrimp and cook, covered, for about 4 minutes. Season with salt and pepper. Add the hot sauce, parsley, and cilantro and serve immediately.

Pargo asado

ROASTED RED SNAPPER

Serves 4 to 6 • Cooking time: 35 minutes

6 whole garlic cloves, peeled

½ teaspoon salt

1 teaspoon dried oregano

½ cup plus 2 tablespoons fresh
   orange juice

½ cup plus 2 tablespoons fresh
   lime juice

4 pounds red snapper fillets

½ bunch fresh parsley, stems
   removed and leaves chopped fine

1 teaspoon ground cumin

¾ cup olive oil

½ cup white wine

2 baking potatoes, peeled and
   sliced fine

1 medium white onion, sliced fine

1 large red bell pepper, sliced fine

12 green olives, pitted and sliced

2 bay leaves

2 hard-cooked eggs, quartered,
   to garnish

1 Preheat the oven to 400° F. Combine 4 of the garlic cloves, the salt, oregano, ½ cup orange juice, and ½ cup lime juice in a food processor.

2 Place the fish fillets in baking dish and pour in the marinade. Refrigerate for 2 hours.

3 Combine the remaining garlic cloves, 2 tablespoons orange juice, and 2 tablespoons lime juice in a food processor. Pour the sauce into a bowl and add the parsley, cumin, olive oil, and wine. Set aside.

4 Layer the potatoes, onion, bell pepper, and olives in a roasting pan.

5 Remove the fish from the marinade, discarding the remaining marinade. Place the fish over the vegetables and add the sauce and bay leaves.

6 Bring to a boil on the stovetop over a medium heat. Remove, place in the oven and bake for 20 minutes. Garnish with the hard-cooked eggs and serve.

Harina con cangrejo

SOFT CORN PUDDING WITH CRABMEAT

Serves 6 • Cooking time: 45 minutes

2 tablespoons olive oil

1 large white onion, chopped fine

1 medium green bell pepper, chopped fine

1 medium tomato, chopped fine

1 canned chipotle chile, chopped

½ cup dry white wine

1 pound lump crabmeat, picked clean, plus more to garnish

¼ bunch fresh cilantro, stems removed and leaves chopped

Salt and fresh ground black pepper, to season

3 cups chicken broth

3 cups clam juice

3 cups cornmeal

8 ounces cream cheese

Lime wedges, to garnish

1 Heat the olive oil in a large skillet. Over a medium heat, cook the onion, bell pepper, and tomato until soft. Add the chipotle and white wine, and cook until the liquid has almost evaporated. Add the crabmeat and cook for a further 3 minutes.

2 Add the cilantro and season with salt and pepper. Remove from the heat and set aside.

3 Place the chicken broth and clam juice in a large saucepan and bring to a boil. Add the cornmeal and cook over a low heat for about 20 minutes, while stirring continuously. Increase the heat to medium and add the cream cheese, being sure to stir thoroughly. Cook for a further 10 minutes. Serve topped with crabmeat and garnish with lime wedges.

Frituras de pescado

FISH FRITTERS

Serves 6 to 8 • Cooking time: 10 minutes

1¼ cups all-purpose flour

1½ teaspoons baking powder

1 teaspoon salt

1 medium egg, beaten

¾ cup milk

1 tablespoon dry white wine

⅓ cup cooked white rice

1½ cups canned tuna, drained

Vegetable oil, for frying

1 Sift the flour, baking powder, and salt into a mixing bowl.

2 In a separate bowl, combine the egg, milk, and wine. Add to the flour mixture. Add the rice and tuna, and mix thoroughly.

3 Pour 1 inch of vegetable oil into a skillet and heat until it reaches 350° F on a frying thermometer. Using a large tablespoon, shape the fritters and drop them into the hot oil. Fry until golden brown on both sides.

Langosta Criolla

CUBAN-STYLE LOBSTER

Serves 4 • Cooking time: 20 minutes

6 tablespoons olive oil

1 small white onion, diced

1 large red bell pepper, diced

3 garlic cloves, chopped fine

4 spiny (rock) lobster tails, cut
  into 1 ½-inch rounds

One 10-ounce can whole
  tomatoes, chopped

1 tablespoon tomato paste

1 bay leaf

1 cup sherry

½ cup roasted red bell pepper
  (about 2 peppers), diced

1 dried ancho chile

1 tablespoon Worcestershire sauce

¼ bunch fresh cilantro, stems
  removed and chopped

Fresh bread, to serve

Lime wedges, to garnish

1 Heat the oil in a large sauté pan and cook the onion, bell pepper, and garlic for about 4 minutes over a medium heat. Add the lobster, tomatoes, tomato paste, and bay leaf and cook for 5 minutes.

2 Deglaze the pan with the sherry. Add the roasted pepper, ancho chile, Worcestershire sauce and cilantro and cook a further 5 minutes. Serve in shallow bowls with fresh bread and garnish with lime wedges.

Pulpo a la gallega

OCTOPUS, GALICIAN STYLE

Serves 4 • Cooking time: 1¾ hours

1 gallon water, salted

1 lemon, cut in half

1 medium white onion, peeled
   and cut in half

2 bay leaves

1 bunch fresh parsley, half left
   whole, and half stems removed
   and leaves chopped

2 tablespoons hot red pepper sauce

One 6- to 8-pound octopus (hold it
   by the tentacles and bang it
   against the countertop several
   times to tenderize it)

2 medium baking potatoes, washed

¼ cup olive oil

3 cloves garlic, peeled and sliced

½ medium white onion, sliced fine

3 teaspoons paprika

1 small bunch fresh parsley,
   chopped fine

Salt and fresh ground black
   pepper, to season

1 Combine the water, lemon halves, onion halves, bay leaves, whole parsley stems, hot sauce, and octopus in a large stockpot and bring to a boil over a high heat. Cook for about 1½ hours or until the octopus is tender. During the last 30 minutes, add the potatoes.

2 Remove the potatoes and set aside to let cool until room temperature. Remove the octopus and let cool for a few minutes.

3 Peel the octopus, which must be done while it is still hot, and completely remove all the ink and the suction cups. Do not rinse the octopus during this process. Keep a bowl of ice water nearby to use to cool your hands. Cut the peeled octopus into 1½-inch pieces and set aside.

4 Peel the potatoes and cut into 2-inch cubes. Heat the olive oil in a medium sauté pan and cook the garlic over a medium heat. Add the onion, potatoes, and octopus. Add the paprika and chopped parsley. Mix well and season with salt and pepper.

Escabeche de bonito

PICKLED TUNA

Serves: 4 • Cooking time: 15 minutes plus overnight marinating

½ cup white vinegar

¾ cup extra virgin olive oil

2 medium white onions, sliced fine

1 medium green bell pepper, sliced fine

¼ cup capers

½ teaspoon paprika

10 large green olives, pitted and sliced

2 tablespoons olive oil

3 pounds bonito tuna, cleaned, deboned, and cut into 1-inch slices

2 garlic cloves, sliced fine

Salt and fresh ground black pepper, to season

Lemon wedges, to garnish

1 Combine the vinegar, olive oil, onions, bell pepper, capers, paprika, and olives in a mixing bowl. Set aside.

2 Heat the 2 tablespoons olive oil in a medium sauté pan, and cook the tuna and garlic for two minutes on each side. Set aside.

3 Add the marinade from Step 1 and cook for 4 minutes. Remove from the heat and season with salt and pepper. Place in the refrigerator and marinate overnight before serving, garnished with lemon wedges.

Meat and poultry

Pernil asado

ROASTED HAM

Serves 8 • Cooking time: about 3 hours plus overnight marinating

¼ cup dried oregano

¾ cup fresh bitter orange juice

¼ cup garlic, peeled and
  chopped fine

¼ cup extra virgin olive oil

One 6- to 8-pound fresh ham

10 whole garlic cloves, peeled

Coarse salt and fresh ground
  black pepper, to season

8 ounces lard

Orange wedges and fresh oregano,
  to garnish

1 Combine the oregano, sour orange juice, garlic, and olive oil in a mixing bowl to make a marinade and set aside.

2 Place the ham on a flat surface, skin-side down. With a sharp knife, make shallow cuts in the meat without piercing through the skin. Stuff the holes with the whole garlic cloves.

3 Rub the marinade all over the meat and season generously with salt and pepper. Let the ham marinate in the refrigerator overnight.

4 The next day, remove the ham from the refrigerator. Preheat the oven to 350° F.

5 Place the ham in a deep roasting pan. Add the lard and enough water to cover the bottom of the pan, about 1 inch. Roast, covered, for about 2 hours, or until the internal temperature reaches 150° F. Remove the cover and cook for a further 30 minutes, or until the internal temperature reaches 160° F. Garnish with orange wedges and fresh oregano. Ideal served with Tostones y maduros (*see* page 118), or boiled or fried yuca.

Chilindrón de cordero

LAMB AND ROASTED PEPPER STEW

Serves 4 • Cooking time: 3 hours 30 minutes

Olive oil, for cooking
One 3-pound lamb shoulder
1 cup chopped white onions
4 garlic cloves, chopped fine
4 ounces Serrano ham, sliced
1 cup drained pequillo peppers
1 cup dry (fino) or semi-dry
  (amontillado) sherry

1 cup ruby port
1 cup dry white wine
One 10-ounce can whole tomatoes
1 bay leaf
2 sprigs fresh rosemary
Fresh rice and red beans,
  to serve.

1 Coat the bottom of a large saucepan with olive oil and heat. Add the lamb and brown on all sides. Remove the lamb from the pan and add the onions, garlic, and ham. Cook until the vegetables become soft.

2 Add the pequillo peppers; deglaze the pan by adding the sherry, port, and white wine. Bring to a boil then reduce the heat and simmer until the mixture is reduced by half.

3 Return the lamb to the pan and add the tomatoes, bay leaf, and rosemary. Simmer for 3 hours and serve with fresh rice and red beans.

Albondigas

CUBAN MEATBALLS

Serves 4 • Cooking time: 1 hour

1½ pounds ground beef
½ small white onion, grated
½ small green bell pepper,
   chopped fine
2 garlic cloves, chopped fine
1 teaspoon ground cumin
1 teaspoon dried oregano
Pinch fresh ground black pepper

¼ teaspoon salt
1 medium egg
½ cup milk
2 slices bread, torn into
   small pieces
Vegetable oil, for frying
4 cups Salsa de tomate
   Cubana (*see* page 64)

1 Combine the ground beef, onion, bell pepper, garlic, cumin, oregano, black pepper, and salt in a mixing bowl.

2 In a separate bowl, beat the egg and milk together. Dip the bread in the egg-milk mixture until soaked through.

3 Add the soaked bread to the beef and mix, using your hands. Shape the beef into medium round balls. Refrigerate the meatballs for about 1 hour.

4 Coat the bottom of a skillet with the vegetable oil and, over a high heat, sear the meatballs on all sides until they are golden brown.

5 Meanwhile, heat the Salsa de tomate Cubana in a medium saucepan. Add the meatballs and cook over a low heat, covered, for about 45 minutes. Serve with fresh pasta.

Picadillo santiaguero

CUBAN-STYLE GROUND BEEF

Serves 4 • Cooking time: 45 minutes

1½ pounds top choice ground beef

1 teaspoon dried oregano

1 teaspoon ground cumin

¼ cup olive oil

2 garlic cloves, chopped fine

1 medium white onion,
   chopped fine

1 small green bell pepper,
   chopped fine

½ cup dry white wine

1 cup tomato sauce

1 medium baking potato, peeled
   and cut into small cubes

8 green olives, pitted and sliced

¼ cup raisins

Salt and fresh ground black
   pepper, to season

1 Thoroughly combine the beef, oregano, and cumin in a mixing bowl.

2 Heat the olive oil in a skillet and cook the garlic, onion, and bell pepper until soft. Add the meat, wine, and tomato sauce. Cover and cook over a medium to low heat for about 15 minutes.

3 Add the potato, cover, and cook for a further 15 minutes. Add the olives and raisins and cook, uncovered, for a further 15 minutes, or until the liquid is almost fully reduced, making sure that the meat is still moist. Season with salt and pepper.

Chuletas de cerdo al estilo Cubano

CUBAN-STYLE PORK CHOPS

Serves 4 • Cooking time: 45 minutes

¼ cup olive oil

3 pounds smoked pork chops,
  each ½ inch thick

1 large white onion, diced

2 medium **Cubanelle** or Italian
  frying peppers, diced

2 roasted red bell peppers, diced

2 garlic cloves, chopped

1 bay leaf

½ cup dry white wine

1 teaspoon white vinegar

3 tablespoons tomato paste

Salt and fresh ground black
  pepper, to season

¼ bunch parsley, stems removed
  and leaves chopped

1 Preheat the oven to 350° F. Heat the oil in a medium skillet and sear the pork chops, for about 1 minute per side. Remove the pork chops and place in a roasting pan. Set aside.

2 In the same skillet, fry the onion, Cubanelle peppers, roasted peppers, garlic, and bay leaf, and cook until the vegetables start to soften. Add the wine and vinegar and bring to a boil. Stir in the tomato paste. Season with salt and pepper. Add the parsley and pour the sauce over the pork chops. Roast for about 20 minutes. Ideal served with Moros y cristianos (*see* page 131) or Congris oriental (*see* page 134).

Caldosa

CALDOSA STEW

Serves 6 • Cooking time: 1 hour

Olive oil, for cooking
½ whole chicken, cut into 4 pieces
8 ounces ham, diced
1 white onion, chopped fine
1 medium Cubanelle or Italian
   frying pepper, chopped fine
2 cloves garlic, chopped
1 pound shrimp, peeled, cleaned,
   and deveined

1 teaspoon Worcestershire sauce
¼ teaspoon paprika
1 bay leaf
½ cup dry white wine
1 tablespoon white vinegar
4 medium tomatoes, chopped
1⅓ cups white rice
2½ cups chicken broth

1 Coat the bottom of a skillet with oil and heat. Cook the chicken until golden brown, for about 10 minutes. Add the ham and cook for 2 minutes followed by the onion, Cubanelle pepper, and garlic, and cook until soft, for about 4 minutes.

2 Season the shrimp with the Worcestershire sauce and paprika, and add to the chicken and ham. Add the bay leaf, wine, vinegar, tomatoes, rice, and chicken broth. Cook, covered, for 30 minutes, or until the rice is soft. The final consistency will be soupy. Can be served with fresh white rice.

Ropa vieja

STEWED SHREDDED BEEF

Serves 4 to 6 • Cooking time: 2¼ hours

**One 2½-pound flank steak,
  cut in half lengthwise**
2 bay leaves
1 carrot, sliced
2 white onions, cut into strips
1 tablespoon dried oregano
**1 medium red bell pepper,
  sliced fine**
**1 medium green bell pepper,
  sliced fine**

2 garlic cloves, chopped
2 tablespoons olive oil
½ cup dry sherry
2 cups whole canned tomatoes
1 teaspoon ground cumin
**Salt and fresh ground black
  pepper, to season**

1 Place the steak, bay leaves, carrot, 1 of the onions, and the oregano in a large saucepan. Cover with water and bring to a boil then simmer for 1 to 1½ hours. Drain the meat and let cool. Cut the meat into 2-inch cubes, and, using your hands, shred the meat.

2 Cook the remaining onion, bell peppers, and garlic in the olive oil in a skillet until soft. Add the sherry to deglaze the pan followed by the tomatoes and cumin, and cook for 15 minutes.

3 Add the shredded meat and cook for a further 30 minutes. Season with salt and pepper and serve with Cuban rice.

Carne mechada

CUBAN-STYLE BEEF STEW

Serves 4 • Cooking time: 2 hours plus 3 hours marinating

Juice of 1 sour orange

1 clove garlic, chopped fine

One 3-pound beef eye round
   (cut from the round steak section
   of the hind quarters), cleaned

6 tablespoons olive oil

4 ounces ham, cut into
   ½-inch pieces

3 slices bacon, diced

2 large white onions, chopped fine

2 medium Cubanelle or Italian

frying peppers, chopped fine

¼ cup tomato paste

¼ bunch parsley, stems removed
   and reserved, and leaves
   chopped

Salt and fresh ground black
   pepper, to season

3 bay leaves

1 cup red wine

Parsley, to garnish

1 Combine the sour orange juice and garlic in a mixing bowl and set aside.

2 With a sharp knife, carefully make lengthwise slits into the two ends of the meat to create pockets for stuffing, being sure to make the slits big enough. Place the meat in a baking pan and cover with the orange juice marinade. Marinate in the refrigerator for 2 to 3 hours.

3 Heat 3 tablespoons of the olive oil in a skillet. Cook the ham and bacon until brown. Add the onions and Cubanelle peppers and cook for a further 3 minutes. Stir in the tomato paste and cook for a further 2 minutes. Add the chopped parsley and stir. Let cool to room temperature.

4 Remove the meat from the refrigerator and stuff with the ham and bacon stuffing. Season with salt and pepper. Preheat the oven to 375° F.

5 In a large ovenproof pot, heat the remaining olive oil and sear the meat until browned on all sides. Add the bay leaves, parsley stems, and any leftover stuffing. Add the red wine and roast, covered, for about 1½ hours. Serve sliced with resulting sauce and garnish with parsley. Serve with maduros and fresh white rice.

Vaca frita

CRISPY SHREDDED BEEF

Serves 4 • Cooking time: 25 minutes

3 pounds flank steak

2 bay leaves

1 carrot, cut into 3 pieces

1 medium tomato, cut in half

½ tablespoon cumin

½ tablespoon dried oregano

¼ cup olive oil

1 large Spanish onion, sliced fine

2 tablespoons chopped fresh
   cilantro

¼ cup fresh lime juice

Salt and fresh ground black
   pepper, to season

Fresh parsley, to garnish

1 In a small stock pan, add the meat, bay leaves, carrot, tomato, cumin, and oregano and cover with water. Bring to a boil and then simmer for about 1 hour until the meat becomes tender. Remove from the heat, drain, and shred the meat.

2 Heat a skillet until it is very hot and add $\frac{1}{8}$ cup of the olive oil. Add the shredded meat, being sure to spread it evenly over the pan. Flip the meat and cook until both sides become crispy.

3 In a separate pan, add the remaining olive oil and cook the onion until caramelized. Mix in the meat, cilantro, and lime juice. Season with salt and pepper. Serve, garnished with parsley. Ideal served with tostones.

Bistec a la plancha

PANSEARED BEEF STEAK

Serves 4 • Cooking time: 10 minutes plus 3 hours marinating

4 garlic cloves, chopped fine

Juice of 3 limes

1 tablespoon olive oil

3 pounds beef tenderloin,
  sliced fine

2 white onions, sliced fine

Salt and fresh ground black
  pepper, to season

Olive oil, for cooking

Yuca frita (*see* page 124), to serve

Salad leaves and lime wedges,
  to garnish

1 Combine the garlic, lime juice, and olive oil in a mixing bowl.

2 Arrange the meat on a platter and top with the onions and the lime juice marinade. Marinate for 3 hours in the refrigerator. Remove the meat from the marinade, reserving the marinade and onions. Season to taste with salt and pepper.

3 Heat a very large skillet and coat the bottom with the olive oil. Cook the meat for about 2 minutes per side, being sure that the pan is not crowded—this ensures that the temperature remains very hot throughout the cooking process.

4 Remove the pan from the heat. Transfer the meat to a serving platter and reserve the cooking juices. Add the reserved marinade and onions to the cooking juices and cook for 4 minutes until the onions are caramelized. Remove from the heat and pour the onions and sauce over the meat. Serve with Yuca frita (*see* page 124) and garnish with salad leaves and lime wedges.

Fricasé de conejo

RABBIT FRICASSEE

Serves 4 • Cooking time: 2 hours 10 minutes

¼ cup olive oil

8 rabbit legs

1 Spanish onion, chopped fine

1 medium green bell pepper,
 chopped fine

2 garlic cloves, chopped

1 tablespoon hot paprika

2 bay leaves

1 tablespoon fresh oregano,
 chopped

1 cup canned, drained, and
 chopped whole tomatoes

1 cup dry (fino) sherry

1 cup chicken broth

2 baking potatoes, such as russets,
 cut into large cubes

¼ cup capers

½ cup dried cherries

¼ cup sweet peas, boiled, to serve

¼ bunch fresh parsley, chopped,
 to garnish

1 Heat the oil in a large saucepan. Brown the rabbit legs on both sides. Add the onion, bell pepper, and garlic and cook for 10 minutes. Add the paprika, bay leaves, oregano, tomatoes, sherry, and chicken broth, and cook for 1 hour.

2 Add the potatoes, capers, and dried cherries and cook for a further hour, or until the potatoes are tender. Serve with boiled sweet peas and garnish with parsley.

Tasajo camagueyano

SALT-CURED BEEF

Serves 4 • Cooking time: 1¼ hours plus overnight soaking

1½ pounds dried salt-cured beef

¼ cup olive oil

1 medium white onion,
 chopped fine

2 green Cubanelle or Italian frying
 peppers, chopped fine

2 garlic cloves, chopped fine

2 cups tomato sauce

½ cup white wine

½ cup beef broth

1 tablespoon white vinegar

1 bay leaf

¼ teaspoon ground cumin

¼ teaspoon chopped fresh oregano

Fresh yellow rice, to serve

Fresh oregano, to garnish

1 Cut the beef into 2-inch cubes. Cover with water and soak overnight.

2 The next day, drain the beef. Place the meat in a large stockpot
and cover with water. Bring to a boil and cook until tender, for about
45 minutes, checking the water to be sure it is not too salty (if necessary,
change the water while cooking). Drain the meat and set aside until cool
enough to handle. Shred the meat and set aside.

3 Heat olive oil in a large skillet and cook the onion, Cubanelle peppers,
and garlic until soft. Add the tomato sauce, white wine, beef broth,
vinegar, bay leaf, cumin, and oregano.

4 Add the shredded meat and cook over a low heat, covered, for about
25 minutes. Cook for a further 5 minutes, uncovered. Serve with yellow
rice and garnish with fresh oregano.

Rabo encendido

OXTAIL STEW

Serves 4 • Cooking time: 3¼ hours

1 cup all-purpose flour

½ cup **Cajun** seasoning

5 pounds oxtails (about 2-inch
 thick rounds)

3 tablespoons olive oil

1 cup tardio, or any dessert wine

1 large **Spanish** onion, diced

2 carrots, diced

3 stalks celery, diced

3 **Cubanelle** or Italian frying
 peppers, cut into large pieces

1 cup **Malbec** red wine

One 10-ounce can whole tomatoes,
 crushed by hand

3 chipotle peppers in adobo

1 cup pisco (a Latin American
 grape brandy, similar to grappa)

3 bay leaves

1 bunch fresh thyme, leaves
 removed and chopped

Salt and fresh ground black
 pepper, to season

Yellow rice, to serve

Sprig of thyme, to garnish

1 Mix the flour and the Cajun seasoning, and coat the oxtails with
the mixture.

2 In a skillet, heat 2 tablespoons of the olive oil. Sear the oxtails on
both sides and remove from the pan. Add half the dessert wine to
deglaze the pan, reserving the other half for later use.

3 In a separate saucepan, heat the remaining olive oil and cook the
onion, carrots, celery, and Cubanelle peppers until the vegetables
caramelize. Add the Malbec to deglaze the pan.

4 Add the oxtail to the vegetables along with the reserved dessert wine.
Add the tomatoes, chipotle, pisco, bay leaves, and thyme. Let simmer
over a low heat for about 3 hours. Season with salt and pepper. Serve
with yellow rice and garnish with a sprig of thyme.

Salpicón de jamón

SLOW-COOKED CUBAN HAM WITH SHERRY VINEGAR

Serves 6 • Cooking time: 1 hour 50 minutes

Olive oil, for cooking

2 carrots, sliced thick

2 white onions, quartered

3 tablespoons tomato paste

2 pounds fresh ham, cut
   into 2-inch pieces

2 pounds smoked ham, cut
   into 2-inch pieces

2 bay leaves

1 cup white wine

10 plum (roma) tomatoes,
   quartered lengthwise

2 medium white onions, sliced fine

4 garlic cloves, sliced

One 10-ounce can peeled whole
   tomatoes, crushed by hand

1 cup sun-dried tomatoes,
   sliced fine

¼ cup sherry vinegar

Salt and fresh ground black
   pepper, to season

Fried plantain, to serve

1 Coat the bottom of a large saucepan with olive oil and cook the carrots and the onions until soft. Stir in the tomato paste and cook until it caramelizes

2 Add the fresh and smoked ham. Add enough water to cover the bay leaves, and the wine. Bring the mixture to a boil then simmer until the meat is very tender, for about 1½ hours, adding more water as needed. Remove from the heat and strain the mixture, reserving the liquor. Shred the meat and set aside.

3 Coat the bottom of a medium skillet with olive oil and cook the plum tomatoes and sliced onions for about 4 minutes, or until translucent. Add the garlic followed by the canned tomatoes, sun-dried tomatoes, and vinegar. Cook for 5 minutes.

4 Add the reserved ham and cook over a low heat for 15 minutes. Use the reserved cooking liquor to keep the stew moist at all times. Season with salt and pepper and serve with fried plantain.

Masitas de cerdo fritas

FRIED PORK CHUNKS

Serves 4 • Cooking time: 15 minutes plus overnight marinating

3 pounds pork, fat removed, cut
   into 1½-inch cubes
1 large white onion, cut into
   thin strips

¾ cup sour **Marinado de naranja
   agria** (*see* **page 67**)
Salt, to season
Vegetable oil, for frying

1 Combine the pork, onion, and Marinado de naranja agria in a mixing bowl. Marinate in the refrigerator overnight. The following day, remove the pork and onion from the marinade. Season with salt and set aside.

2 Coat the bottom of a skillet with a 1-inch layer of vegetable oil. Over a medium heat, heat the oil and add the pork and onions, and cook through, for about 6 minutes.

3 Turn up heat and turn the pork several times until the meat is crispy and brown on all sides. Ideal served with tostones.

Accompaniments and rice dishes

Tostones y maduros

FRIED SWEET AND GREEN PLANTAINS

Serves 4 • Cooking time: 15 minutes plus 2 hours soaking

For the tostones and maduros
Vegetable oil, for frying
2 large ripe plantains (maduros),
    peeled and sliced at an angle
2 large green plantains (tostones),
    peeled and cut into 1½-inch
    rounds

For the pickled red onions
1 red onion, sliced fine into rings
½ cup fresh lime juice

1 Pour about 1 inch of vegetable oil into a skillet. Heat to a very high temperature.

2 To make the maduros, fry the ripe plantains until golden on both sides, being sure to turn them several times. Transfer to a dish.

3 To make the tostones, fry the green plantains for about 8 minutes, or until soft all the way through, being sure to turn them several times. Transfer to the dish with the ripe plantains. Place a wet towel over them, and pressing down with your hands, smash the plantains.

4 Return the oil to a very high temperature and fry the smashed plantains again until crispy on both sides. Arrange the tostones and maduros on a serving platter.

5 To make the pickled red onions, mix the onion and lime juice together and marinate for a couple of hours. Pour over the plantains and serve.

Frituras de malanga

TARO ROOT FRITTERS

Serves: 4 to 6 • Cooking time: 10 to 15 minutes

1 pound peeled malanga
  (taro root), grated
½ teaspoon salt
⅛ bunch of fresh parsley, stems
  removed and leaves chopped fine

½ medium white onion, grated
1 medium egg, beaten
Vegetable oil, for frying
Fresh parsley, to garnish

1 Combine the taro, salt, parsley, and onion in a bowl. Add the beaten egg and mix until thoroughly combined.

2 Heat the vegetable oil in a skillet until it reaches 350° F on a frying thermometer. Use a tablespoon to shape the mixture into fritters the size of the spoon. Fry the fritters until crispy and golden brown on all sides. Serve, garnished with fresh parsley.

Fufú de plátanos moderno

SWEET PLANTAIN MASH

Serves 4 to 6 • Cooking time: 30 minutes

8 sweet plantains (be sure they are not too ripe), peeled and cut into 2-inch slices

1 large white onion, chopped fine
12 ounces bacon, chopped fine

1 Place the plantains in a large saucepan and cover with water. Bring to a boil and cook until tender, for about 25 minutes. Drain the plantains and mash with a food mill.

2 Cook the onion and the bacon in a skillet until the fat renders, for about 5 minutes. Add the bacon-onion mixture to the purée and mix thoroughly

Mazorca carboncilla

GRILLED CORN ON COB

Serves 6 • Cooking time: 30 minutes

6 ears corn in the husks, with only the darkest outer green leaves removed

Salted butter, to serve
Salt, to season

1 Dip the corn ears in water, being sure to wet the husks.

2 Cook the corn on the grill until tender, for about 25 minutes; while cooking, you will see some steam and a little smoke.

3 Remove from the grill and carefully peel the husks back. Using the end of the corn as a handle, return the corn to the grill and cook, continuously rotating, for a further 5 minutes. To serve, brush with butter and season with salt.

Asopado de mariscos

SEAFOOD STEW

Serves 6 • Cooking time: 3 hours

Olive oil, for cooking
1 medium white onion, chopped
1 medium green bell pepper, chopped
Two 1½-pound lobsters, heads removed and reserved (tail in shell sliced into 1-inch thick pieces, and claws cracked)
8 ounces large shrimp, peeled, cleaned, and deveined, shells reserved
1 cup canned tomato sauce
1 cup dry white wine
2 bay leaves, divided

4 cups clam juice
4 cups water
1 medium white onion, chopped fine
1 medium green bell pepper, chopped fine
2 cups white short grain rice
24 Little Neck clams, cleaned
24 mussels, cleaned
Pinch saffron
8 ounces sea scallops, cleaned
½ bunch culantro, chopped fine
Salt and fresh ground black pepper, to season

1 Add enough olive oil to thinly coat the bottom of a large saucepan. Cook the onion and bell pepper until soft.

2 Add the lobster heads and shrimp shells and cook until the shells of both begin to turn red. Add the tomato sauce, white wine, and 1 of the bay leaves. Add the clam juice and water and cook for at least 2 hours. Strain and reserve the seafood broth.

3 Coat the bottom of a medium saucepan with olive oil and cook the onion and bell pepper until soft. Add the rice, clams, mussels, 1 bay leaf, and pinch of saffron. Pour in the reserved seafood broth and cook until the rice is soft, for about 20 minutes.

4 Add the shrimp, scallops, and lobster, and cook for about 8 minutes. Finally add the culantro and season with salt and pepper.

Yuca frita

CRISPY YUCA STICKS

Serves 4 • Cooking time: 45 minutes

4 medium yucas, peeled, or
 1 pack frozen yuca, cut
 into 2-inch pieces
¼ cup extra virgin olive oil
6 garlic cloves, crushed
1 large Spanish onion, diced small
Vegetable oil, for frying

½ cup bitter orange juice, or ⅛ cup
 fresh orange juice and ⅛ cup
 fresh lime juice combined
1 tablespoon fresh cilantro
Salt, to season

1 Place the yuca in a saucepan, cover with water, and boil until tender, for about 30 minutes. Drain and set aside.

2 In a small saucepan, heat the olive oil, garlic, and onion until fragrant. Remove the seasoned olive oil and set aside in a small mixing bowl to cool.

3 Pour 1 inch of vegetable oil into a skillet and heat to a very high temperature. Fry the yuca until crisp and brown, being sure to turn the pieces over several times. Remove from the pan and place in a bowl.

4 Combine the orange juice, cilantro, and reserved seasoned olive oil to make a mojo. Toss the yuca in the mojo and season with salt to taste.

Yuca con mojo

YUCAS IN HOT GARLIC SAUCE

Serves 4 • Cooking time: 45 minutes

4 medium yucas, peeled, or
   1 pack frozen yuca, cut
   into 1½-inch pieces
4 large Spanish onions, sliced fine
½ cup bitter orange juice, or ⅛ cup
   fresh orange juice and ⅛ cup
   fresh lime juice combined

1 tablespoon fresh cilantro
6 garlic cloves, crushed
¼ cup extra virgin olive oil
Orange wedges, to garnish

1 Place the yuca in a saucepan,
cover with water, and boil until
tender, for about 30 minutes.
Drain, place in a bowl, and
set aside.

2 Mix the onions, bitter orange
juice, cilantro, and garlic in
a small bowl and pour over
the yuca.

3 Heat the oil in a skillet until it
is very hot (but does not smoke).
Pour the hot oil over the yuca.

Arroz amarillo

SPANISH RICE

Serves 4 • Cooking time: 35 minutes

4 tablespoons olive oil

1 Spanish onion, diced

4 cups white long-grain rice

6 cups water

Salt, to season

2 bay leaves

¼ teaspoon bijol (turmeric)

1 Heat the olive oil in a medium saucepan over a medium heat. Add the onion and cook until soft. Add the rice, stirring, until coated with the oil.

2 Add the water and bring to a boil. Season generously with salt and add the bay leaves and bijol. Cook over a medium heat, uncovered, for about 20 minutes, until most of the water has been absorbed by the rice.

Arroz con pollo

CUBAN-STYLE CHICKEN-FLAVORED RICE

Serves 6 to 8 • Cooking time: 45 minutes

Olive oil, for cooking

One 3-pound whole chicken, cut
into 8 pieces

1 large white onion, chopped fine

1 green bell pepper, chopped fine

2 cloves garlic, chopped fine

½ cup **Salsa de tomate Cubana**
(*see* page 64), or canned tomato
sauce

½ cup dry white wine

4 cups water

½ teaspoon salt

½ teaspoon ground cumin

½ teaspoon dried oregano

1 bay leaf

½ teaspoon bijol (turmeric), or
½ teaspoon saffron

5 cups white long-grain rice

12 fluid ounces beer

1 cup frozen sweet peas

3 roasted red bell peppers, diced

¼ cup extra virgin olive oil

1 Coat the bottom of a large saucepan with olive oil and heat over a high heat. Add the chicken, onion, bell pepper, and garlic and cook until the chicken pieces are golden brown.

2 Add the tomato sauce, wine, and water and bring to a boil over medium heat. Stir in the salt, cumin, oregano, bay leaf, and bijol, and then add the rice. Continue to cook over a medium heat, uncovered, until most of the liquor has been absorbed by the rice.

3 Add the beer, peas, and roasted peppers. Cook, covered, for a further 20 minutes, or until the rice is tender. Remove from the heat and add the extra virgin olive oil. Let stand for 10 minutes before serving.

Arroz con gandules

PIGEON PEA RICE

Serves 8 to 10 • Cooking time: 1 hour

6 strips bacon, diced
1 large white onion, chopped
2 Cubanelle or Italian frying
   peppers, diced
2 garlic cloves, chopped fine
1 pound ham, diced
3 tablespoons tomato paste

Two 15-ounce cans pigeon peas
6 cups chicken broth
Salt, to season
6 cups Canilla rice
Banana leaves (optional)

1 Cook the bacon in a skillet and drain the fat. Add in the onion, Cubanelle peppers, and garlic and cook over a medium heat until the vegetables are golden brown. Add the ham. Stir in the tomato paste and let it caramelize.

2 Add the pigeon peas and chicken broth and season with salt. Bring the mixture to a boil and stir in the rice. Cook over a medium heat until the rice has absorbed most of the liquid.

3 Cover with banana leaves (optional) or a lid, and continue cooking over a very low heat until the rest of the liquid has been absorbed, for about 20 minutes.

Pionono

SWEET PLANTAIN AND BEEF CAKES

Serves 6 • Cooking time: 15 minutes

Vegetable oil, for frying
**4 sweet plantains, peeled and
    sliced lengthwise into 3 pieces**
Toothpicks
**2 cups Picadillo santiaguero
    (*see* page 99)**

4 medium eggs, beaten
1 cup cracker meal
Fresh parsley, to garnish

1 Heat 1 inch of vegetable oil in a large skillet to about 375° F. Fry the plantains, turning them often, until both sides are golden.

2 On a flat surface, use 2 plantain slices to form a hollow circle, holding the slices together with toothpicks. The circle should fit perfectly on the surface of a spatula. Repeat with all the slices, making 6 circles.

3 Tightly pack the picadillo into the center of each circle to form a patty, with the plantain slices as the outer edges. Using the spatula, pick up each patty, one at a time, and carefully dip into the eggs and then the cracker meal, coating both sides.

4 Fry the patties until golden brown, for about 1 minute per side. Serve garnished with fresh parsley.

Moros y cristianos

RICE AND RED BEANS

Serves 6 • Cooking time: 2 hours

½ pound dried navy beans

1 Cubanelle or Italian frying
pepper, cut in half

1 bay leaf

4 ounces bacon, diced

4 ounces ham, chopped fine

¼ cup olive oil

1 medium white onion,
chopped fine

1 medium green bell pepper,
chopped fine

2 garlic cloves, peeled and
chopped fine

1 tablespoon tomato paste

1 teaspoon dried oregano

1 teaspoon ground cumin

2 cups white long-grain rice

Salt, to season

1 Combine the beans with the Cubanelle pepper and bay leaf in a large saucepan. Cover with water, being sure there are about 2 inches of water over the beans. Cover and bring to a boil, and cook until the beans are tender, for about 1½ hours. Drain, reserving 3 cups of the cooking liquor

2 Add the bacon and ham to a large saucepan. Cook until the fat begins to render from the meat Add the olive oil, onion, bell pepper, and garlic and cook until soft. Stir in the tomato paste and allow it to caramelize.

3 Add the beans, reserved cooking liquor, oregano, cumin, and rice. Season with salt. Bring to a boil, cover, and cook at a very low heat for about 20 minutes. Fluff with a fork before serving.

Hallacas vegetarianas

VEGETARIAN TAMALES

Serves 5 to 6 • Cooking time: 1 hour

12 ears of corn, husked and silks
   removed, with husks reserved
Olive oil, for cooking
3 cloves garlic, chopped fine
1 large white onion, chopped fine
1 medium green bell pepper,
   chopped fine

½ cup canned tomato sauce
2 tablespoons cornstarch
Salt and fresh ground black
   pepper, to season

1 Remove the kernels from the cobs, scraping the cobs to extract the corn "milk." Set aside.

2 Make a sofrito by coating the bottom of a skillet with olive oil and cooking the garlic, onion, and bell pepper until soft, for about 4 minutes. Add the tomato sauce and cook until the liquor has evaporated, for about 5 minutes.

3 Blend the corn kernels, corn milk, and sofrito in a food processor. Add the cornstarch and purée until smooth. Season with salt and pepper.

4 Place 2 corn husks side-by-side (overlapping in the center), with the pointy ends on the outside. Spoon 2 tablespoons of the corn mixture in the middle of the corn husks. Fold both ends of the corn husks in toward the middle and tie the ends securely with string. Boil in salted water for 45 minutes.

Congris oriental

RICE AND BLACK BEANS

Serves 4 • Cooking time: 45 minutes plus overnight soaking

8 ounces dried black beans

5 cups fresh water

1 bay leaf

½ Cubanelle or Italian
    frying pepper

Olive oil, for frying

1 medium white onion,
    chopped fine

1 medium Cubanelle or Italian
    frying pepper, diced

2 garlic cloves, chopped

½ teaspoon dried oregano

2 cups white long-grain rice

Salt, to season

2 garlic cloves, crushed

4 tablespoons olive oil

White vinegar, to season

1 Soak the beans in some water overnight. Drain and discard the water.

2 The following day, combine the fresh water, beans, bay leaf, and the half Cubanelle pepper in a large saucepan and bring to a full boil. Reduce the heat and simmer, covered, until the beans are tender. Strain and remove the pepper, reserving the cooking liquor (if necessary add more water to the cooking liquor to make 4 cups).

3 Coat the bottom of a large saucepan with olive oil and cook the onion, Cubanelle pepper, garlic, and oregano for about 4 minutes or until translucent.

4 Add the rice, beans, reserved cooking liquor, and salt, and bring to a boil. Reduce the heat and cook, covered, until the rice is soft.

5 In a separate pan, cook the crushed garlic in the 4 tablespoons of olive oil until it browns. Remove the garlic and add it to the rice. Season with vinegar to taste and let stand for at least an hour before serving.

Arroz Cubano

CUBAN-STYLE WHITE RICE

Serves 4 • Cooking time: 45 minutes

**One 2-inch piece of tocino (fat
back), cut into 4 pieces**
4 tablespoons olive oil
4 cups white long-grain rice

6 cups water
Salt, to season
2 bay leaves

1 Cook the tocino in the olive oil in a medium saucepan until the fat begins to render. Add the rice, stirring, until coated with the oil.

2 Add the water and bring to a boil. Season generously with salt and add the bay leaves. Cook, uncovered, over a medium heat until most of the water has been absorbed by the rice, stirring regularly. Then cover and cook over a very low heat until the rice is tender, for about 20 minutes.

Platános en tentación

ROASTED SWEET PLANTAINS

Serves 4 • Cooking time: 20 minutes

1 cup sugar
¼ cup ground cinnamon

**4 sweet plantains, peeled and
cut in half lengthwise**

1 Preheat the oven to 190°C/375°F. Combine the sugar and cinnamon in a mixing bowl. Coat the plantains with the sugar-cinnamon mixture.

2 Bake in a baking dish for approximately 20 minutes.

Opposite: Platános en tentación

Pan de boniato

CUBAN WHITE SWEET POTATO MUFFINS

Serves 6 to 8 • Cooking time: 55 minutes

1½ cups all-purpose flour

1 tablespoon sugar

5 teaspoons baking powder

½ teaspoon salt

2 medium eggs

1 cup milk

About 4 boniatos (Cuban white sweet potatoes), boiled and mashed (1 cup of purée)

4 ounces (1 stick) melted butter

1 Preheat the oven to 400° F. Grease and lightly flour a 2-pound loaf tin.

2 Sift together the flour, sugar, baking powder, and salt three times. Set aside.

3 In a separate bowl, beat the eggs and gradually beat in the milk. Whisk in the boniato purée until all the ingredients are incorporated. Combine the flour and boniato mixture, then add the melted butter, being sure not to over mix.

4 Fill the loaf tin with the mixture and bake for 55 minutes.

Desserts

Boniato anaranjado

ORANGE-SCENTED CANDIED SWEET POTATO

Serves 4 • Cooking time: 1 hour

**4 boniatos (Cuban white sweet
  potatoes), peeled and cut into
  medium cubes
Zest and juice of 1 orange
½ cup white cane sugar**

**4 medium egg yolks
2 tablespoons dry white wine
1 tablespoon unsalted butter
Ground cinnamon, orange zest,
  and wedges, to garnish**

1 Place the boniatos in a large saucepan. Cover with water and bring to a boil. Cook until tender, for about 20 minutes. Remove from the heat and drain, reserving the cooking water.

2 Purée the boniatos in a blender, using the cooking water as needed to keep the purée moist. Add the orange zest, orange juice, and sugar, and blend until thoroughly combined.

3 Place the purée in a medium saucepan. Bring to a boil, stirring constantly, until the mixture starts to thicken. Remove from the heat and mix in the egg yolks.

4 Return the pan to the heat and add the wine and butter. Continue to cook until the mixture thickens to a medium consistency. Remove from the heat. To serve, garnish with ground cinnamon, orange zest, and wedges.

Pudín de pan

CUBAN BREAD PUDDING

Serves 8 • Cooking time: 1¼ hours

4 cups sugar

Butter, for greasing

1 pound sliced white bread, Cuban bread, or French baguette

4 medium eggs

1 teaspoon vanilla extract

1 teaspoon ground cinnamon

4 ounces (1 stick) melted butter

3 cups milk

¼ teaspoon salt

2 tablespoons dry white wine

2 tablespoons brandy

1 cup raisins

½ cup sliced almonds

1 Preheat the oven to 375° F. Cook 3 cups of the sugar in a saucepan over a medium heat. Stir carefully with a wooden spoon until the sugar caramelizes. Remove from the heat and immediately pour into a greased 9 x 9-inch baking pan. Set aside.

2 Place the bread in a food processor and grind to make medium bread crumbs.

3 In a mixing bowl, combine the eggs, vanilla, cinnamon, melted butter, milk, the remaining sugar, salt, wine, brandy, raisins, and almonds. Add the bread crumbs and mix to thoroughly combine. Pour the mixture into the baking pan. Bake for about 1 hour, or until a knife blade inserted into the center of the pudding comes out clean. Remove from the oven and cool. Serve chilled.

Pasteles de guayaba y queso

GUAVA AND CHEESE TURNOVERS

Makes 12 large or 24 bite-sized turnovers • Cooking time: 25 minutes

1 pound cream cheese
1 pound (4 sticks) unsalted butter,
  softened

4 cups all-purpose flour
1½ pounds guava paste
Sugar, for sprinkling

1 Blend the cream cheese, butter, and flour until well mixed. Wrap in plastic wrap and refrigerate for at least 30 minutes. Preheat the oven to 375° F.

2 Roll the dough into a ¼-inch thick square. Cut into 12 or 24 squares—12 for larger turnovers, 24 for bite-sized turnovers.

3 Place about 1 tablespoon of guava paste on each square, slightly off-center. Fold the dough over the paste, forming a triangle. Press the edges shut.

4 Place the turnovers on a baking sheet and sprinkle with a thin layer of sugar. Bake until evenly browned on all sides, for about 25 minutes.

Buñuelos de boniato y yuca

CUBAN WHITE SWEET POTATO AND YUCA FRITTERS

Serves 6 • Cooking time: 50 minutes

Water, for cooking
1 pound yuca, peeled and diced
8 ounces boniatos (Cuban white
  sweet potatoes), peeled,
  washed, and diced
8 ounces sweet potatoes, peeled,
  washed, and diced medium
2 small eggs, beaten
½ teaspoon salt

½ teaspoon star anise seeds
All-purpose flour
2 cups sugar
1 cup water
Rind of 1 lemon, grated
Juice of ½ lemon
2 cinnamon sticks
3 star anise
Vegetable oil, for frying

1 Place some water, the yuca, boniatos, and sweet potatoes in a medium stockpot. Bring to a boil and cook until just tender. Remove from the pot and drain.

2 Mash the yuca, boniatos, and sweet potatoes together into a purée by hand. Set aside.

3 Mix the eggs, salt, and star anise seeds, and add to the purée. Add enough flour to create a dough-like consistency. Mold into 1-inch balls and set aside.

4 Place the sugar, water, lemon rind, lemon juice, cinnamon sticks, and star anise in a saucepan and bring to a boil. When all ingredients are combined and the sugar has dissolved, remove from the heat. Refrigerate the sugar syrup until chilled.

5 Pour the vegetable oil into a skillet and heat to 375° F on a frying thermometer. Fry the dough balls until golden brown. Remove from the oil and let cool. Serve with the sugar syrup.

Majarete

CORN PUDDING

Serves 4 to 6 • Cooking time: 30 minutes

**10 corn cobs, husked and
  silks removed**
1 quart milk
2 cups sugar

**1 teaspoon ground cinnamon,
  plus more to garnish**
Salt, to taste

1 Carefully cut the corn kernels from the cobs.

2 Combine the corn and half the milk in a blender. Strain the mixture through a fine mesh strainer, pushing down with a ladle or large serving spoon to extract the liquid from the corn kernels.

3 Add the remaining milk, sugar, cinnamon, and salt to taste to the strained mixture and cook it in a saucepan over a low heat, stirring constantly, until creamy.

4 To serve, pour onto a platter and garnish with ground cinnamon.

Dulce de leche

CARAMELIZED MILK

Serves 8 • Cooking time: 3 hours

1 gallon milk
3 cups sugar
3 tablespoons white vinegar

**Queso blanco or cream cheese
  and/or caramelized fruits**

1 Place the milk and sugar in a large saucepan. Bring to a boil.

2 Add the vinegar, which will cause the milk-sugar mixture to separate, and cook until the liquid has evaporated and the solids have caramelized, for about 3 hours. Serve cold with queso blanco and/or caramelized fruits.

Dulce de cascaras

CANDIED CITRUS RIND

Serves 6 to 8 • Cooking time: 2 hours plus 24 hours soaking

3 large ripe grapefruits	**2 cups sugar**
Water	**4 cups water**
Salt	**Gouda or cream cheese, to serve**

1 Quarter and peel the grapefruits, being sure to remove as much of the bitter white pith as possible. Cover the shells in cold, salted water for 24 hours, changing the water regularly to remove bitterness.

2 The following day drain the shells and discard the soaking water. Place the shells into a large saucepan with fresh, cold water to cover and bring to a boil over a medium to high heat. Discard the water as soon as it reaches a boil and repeat the procedure.

3 Drain the shells and pat them dry with paper towels to remove all the moisture. Place them in a large saucepan with the sugar and 4 cups water and cook over a low heat, uncovered, until the shells are soft and transparent and the syrup has thickened, for about 1½ to 2 hours.

4 Let the shells and syrup cool to room temperature. Transfer to a bowl and refrigerate, covered, until ready to serve. Serve chilled with Gouda or cream cheese.

Turrón de coco

COCONUT MACAROONS

Serves 4 to 6 • Cooking time: 25 minutes

Butter or cooking spray,
  for greasing
4 medium eggs
½ cup sugar
Zest of 1 lemon

1½ cups sweetened shredded
  coconut
⅓ cup all-purpose flour
4 ounces (1 stick) butter, melted

1 Preheat the oven to 350° F. Grease a baking sheet with cooking spray or butter.

2 Beat the eggs and sugar in a mixing bowl until the mixture doubles in volume. Mix in the lemon zest.

3 In a separate mixing bowl, combine the coconut, flour, and melted butter. Add the coconut mixture to the eggs and beat thoroughly.

4 Place the mixture in a piping bag without a tip. Squeeze silver-dollar sized dollops onto the baking sheet and bake for 25 minutes.

Dulce de papaya

CARAMELIZED PAPAYA

Serves 4 • Cooking time: 40 minutes

6 cups green papaya, peeled and diced

3 cups packed brown sugar

¼ teaspoon salt

Rind of 1 lemon, grated

3 cinnamon sticks

1 teaspoon vanilla extract

Cream cheese, to serve

Mint leaves, to garnish

1 Place all the ingredients in a large saucepan over a medium heat and cook, covered, for about 30 minutes.

2 Remove the pan from the heat, uncover until the bubbling slows down, and return to the stove. Cook over a low heat until the papaya becomes translucent, then remove from the heat and let cool. Serve chilled with cream cheese and garnish with mint leaves

Churros

Serves 4 • Cooking time: 12 minutes

For the rolls
5 cups water
8 ounces (2 sticks) unsalted butter
2 teaspoons salt
½ cup sugar
2½ cups corn oil
2 teaspoons vanilla extract
1 teaspoon nutmeg
5 cups all-purpose flour
8 medium eggs

For the cinnamon sugar
½ cup sugar
½ cup ground cinnamon

For the chocolate caliente
1 quart milk
8 ounces Mexican chocolate, coarsely chopped
¼ cup sugar

1 In a skillet, heat the water, butter, salt, sugar, ½ cup of corn oil, vanilla, and nutmeg in a saucepan and bring to a rolling boil over a high heat.

2 Reduce to a low heat, mix in the flour, and add the eggs one at a time. Stir vigorously for about 1 minute until the mixture forms a ball. Continue beating until smooth. Remove from the heat and let the dough cool in the pan until room temperature.

3 Place the dough in a piping bag fitted with a star tip. Heat the remaining 2 cups of corn oil in a large frying pan to 375° F. Pipe the dough in long rod shapes directly into the hot oil. Fry until golden brown on all sides and set aside to cool to room temperature.

4 To make the cinnamon sugar, mix the sugar and cinnamon together in a small bowl. Store in an airtight container.

5 To make the chocolate caliente, bring the milk to a boil in a saucepan. Add the chocolate and sugar, and stir over a moderate heat until the chocolate is melted and the sugar has dissolved.

6 When the rolls have cooled, dust them with the cinnamon sugar and serve with chocolate caliente.

Mermelada de mango

MANGO MARMALADE

Serves 4 • Cooking time: 45 minutes

6 large mangoes, peeled and sliced
1 cup water

White sugar
Cream cheese, to serve

1 Place the mangoes and water in a stockpot and bring to a boil.

2 Remove from the heat. Purée the mangoes and the cooking water in a blender. Strain the purée.

3 Weigh the strained purée, place in a saucepan, and add an equal amount of sugar.

4 Cook over a very low heat, stirring regularly to prevent sticking, until the purée comes to a boil and thickens. Remove from the heat and let cool until room temperature. Serve chilled with cream cheese.

Natilla de chocolate

CHOCOLATE PUDDING

Serves 6 • Cooking time: 35 minutes

1 gallon milk
1 cinnamon stick
¼ teaspoon salt
8 medium egg yolks
1½ cups sugar
4 tablespoons all-purpose flour

¼ cup water
8 ounces semi-sweet chocolate
1 teaspoon vanilla
Whipped cream, to serve
Cinnamon sticks, to garnish

1 Place the milk, cinnamon, and salt in a saucepan and bring to a boil. Remove from the heat and set aside.

2 Beat the egg yolks and sugar in a mixing bowl.

Above: Natilla de chocolate

3 In a separate bowl, thoroughly dissolve the flour in the water and add to the yolk mixture. Add the boiled milk and then strain into a saucepan.

4 Place the mixture over a medium heat and add the chocolate, stirring constantly, until the chocolate melts and the mixture becomes thick. Stir in the vanilla. Pour into bowls, let cool to room temperature, and chill until ready to serve. Serve with a little whipped cream and garnish with slivered cinnamon sticks.

Arroz con leche

RICE PUDDING

Serves: 4 • Cooking time: 40 minutes

½ cup white long-grain rice, rinsed

2 cups water

½ teaspoon salt

Rind of 1 lemon, grated

3 cinnamon sticks

One 10-ounce can evaporated milk

1 cup sugar

1 teaspoon vanilla extract

Ground cinnamon, to garnish

1 Cook the rice, water, salt, lemon rind, and cinnamon sticks in a medium saucepan over a medium heat for about 15 minutes.

2 Once the rice begins to split open, add the evaporated milk and sugar. Cook over a very low heat, stirring continuously, until the mixture becomes creamy. Discard the rind and reserve the cinnamon sticks.

3 Remove from the heat and add the vanilla. Chill in individual serving cups and serve garnished with powdered cinnamon and the reserved cinnamon sticks. Ideal served with Mermelada de mango (*see* page 152).

Panetela del trópico

CUBAN POUND CAKE

Serves: 8 to 10 • Cooking time: 45 minutes

3 cups sugar

1 cup water

Rind of 1 lemon, grated

Juice of half a lemon

2 cinnamon sticks

3 star anise

4 medium eggs, separated

1 cup all-purpose flour, sifted

1 large mango, peeled
   and sliced fine

1 small pineapple, peeled and
   sliced fine

1 banana, peeled and sliced
   diagonally

Butter, for greasing

½ cup packed brown sugar

4 ounces (1 stick) unsalted butter

Ground cinnamon, for dusting

1 Place 2 cups of the sugar, water, lemon rind, lemon juice, cinnamon sticks, and star anise in a saucepan and bring to a boil. When all the ingredients are completely combined and the sugar has dissolved, remove from the heat and set the resulting syrup aside. Preheat the oven to 375° F.

2 Place the egg whites in a mixing bowl and beat to an almost meringue-like consistency. Slowly fold in the remaining cup of sugar.

3 Mix the egg yolks into the beaten egg whites one at a time. Slowly add the flour, mixing by hand to thoroughly combine and make a batter.

4 Layer the fruit—first the mango, then the pineapple, and then the banana, in a greased 9 x 9-inch baking pan. Pour the batter over the fruit and bake for about 30 minutes, or until a knife blade stuck into the center of the cake comes out clean. Remove from oven.

5 In a small saucepan, combine the brown sugar and butter, and cook over a medium heat for about 5 minutes until it becomes a syrup.

6 When cool remove the cake from the pan by flipping it over onto a serving platter. Pour the syrup over it and dust with ground cinnamon.

Torrejas

CUBAN SWEET TOAST WITH STAR ANISE SYRUP

Serves 4 to 6 • Cooking time: 40 minutes

For the toast

Day-old French baguette, or other crusty bread, cut into 1-inch thick slices

1 cup milk

¼ cup sugar

½ cup sherry

½ cup port

4 medium eggs, beaten

1 teaspoon ground cinnamon

Vegetable oil, for frying

For the sugar syrup

2 cups sugar

1 cup water

Rind of 1 lemon, grated

Juice of half a lemon

2 cinnamon sticks

3 pieces star anise

Lemon zest, to garnish

1 Spread the bread out on a baking sheet and set aside.

2 Combine the milk and sugar in a mixing bowl. Spoon the milk over each slice of bread, being sure to soak each piece evenly. Repeat with the sherry and then the port.

3 Top the bread with cinnamon and set aside for 10 minutes.

4 Coat the bottom of a frying pan with vegetable oil. Dip the bread in the eggs and fry on both sides over a medium heat until golden brown on both sides, turning once, being careful not to break the pieces. Remove from the heat and set aside to cool to room temperature.

5 To make the sugar syrup, place all the syrup ingredients in a saucepan and bring to a boil over a medium heat. When all the ingredients are completely combined (being sure that the sugar is completely dissolved) remove from the heat and let cool to room temperature. Pour the sugar syrup over the bread and refrigerate until chilled. Serve cold, garnished with lemon zest.

Flan

CUSTARD

Serves 6 to 8 • Cooking time: 1 hour

1 cup sugar

**One 14-fluid-ounce can
condensed milk**

**One 12-fluid-ounce can
evaporated milk**

4 medium eggs

1 teaspoon vanilla extract

1 Preheat the oven to 350° F. Heat a saucepan over a low heat. Add the sugar and stir continuously with a wooden spoon until the sugar has melted and is a light caramel color. Pour the caramel into a 9-inch baking pan and set aside.

2 Combine the condensed milk, evaporated milk, eggs, and vanilla in a blender.

3 Pour the mixture into the pan with the caramel. Place the pan in a larger one containing hot water and bake for about 1 hour or until a knife blade inserted in the middle comes out dry.

4 Remove from the oven, cool to room temperature, and refrigerate for 1 hour before serving. Turn upside down onto a platter to serve.

Coffees and drinks

Café Cubano

Serves 1 • Cooking time: 2 minutes

Cold water
1 tablespoon ground espresso
**   per demitasse cup of water**
**   (3 fluid ounces)**
Sugar

1 Fill the lower chamber of a stovetop espresso maker with fresh cold water, almost all the way up to the small steam valve.

2 Fill the basket with ground espresso, set the basket on top of the lower chamber, and screw the top chamber tightly.

3 Place the espresso maker on a burner and brew over a medium heat until the bubbling sound stops and the top chamber is full. Remove the espresso maker from the heat.

4 Pour the resulting coffee into a demitasse cup to about three-quarters full, leaving enough room for the sugar to be added.

5 Stir in the sugar, mixing well to achieve a frothy top on the espresso.

Café jengibre

Serves 1 • Cooking time: 4 minutes

1 teaspoon ground espresso coffee
¼ teaspoon ground ginger
Cold water
1 cup steaming hot boiled milk
1 teaspoon honey

1 Mix together the ground coffee and ginger.

2 Fill the basket of an espresso maker with the espresso mix and set on top of the lower chamber filled with water. Screw the top chamber tightly and brew over a medium heat until the bubbling stops.

3 Pour the milk into a coffee cup and add the brewed espresso. Stir in the honey.

Opposite: Café Cubano

Above: Café con leche

Café con leche

Serves 1 • Cooking time: 4 minutes

¾ cup steaming hot boiled milk
1 serving freshly brewed Café Cubano
(*see* page 161)
Sugar, to taste

Pour the milk into a coffee cup.
Add one serving of Café Cubano
and sweeten with sugar.

Café flameado

Serves 1 • Cooking time: 2 minutes

¾ cup freshly brewed Café Cubano
(*see* page 161)
1 teaspoon sugar
White rum, to taste

1 Pour the Café Cubano and sugar
into a coffee cup and stir.

2 Pour the rum into a serving spoon
and light, exercising extreme caution.
Pour the lit rum directly into the cup
without putting out the flame.

Above: Rocio de gallo

Rocio de gallo

Serves 1 • Cooking time: 2 minutes

¾ cup freshly brewed **Café Cubano**
    (*see* page 161)
2 fluid ounces white rum
White cane sugar, to taste

Pour the freshly brewed espresso
into a heatproof glass. Add the rum
and sweeten with sugar to taste.

Avispa

Serves 1 • Cooking time: 4 minutes

3 fluid ounces steaming
    hot boiled milk
1 serving freshly brewed **Café Cubano**
    (*see* page 161)
1 teaspoon sugar
2 cloves
1½ fluid ounces white rum

1 Pour the milk into a coffee cup.
Add one serving of Café Cubano.

2 Add the sugar, the cloves, and the
rum. Stir thoroughly and serve.

Above: Bellomonte

Daiquiri

Serves 1

1 fluid ounce fresh lime juice
⅔ fluid ounce simple syrup,
   or 2 ounces white cane sugar
1¾ fluid ounces white Habana Club, or
   other good quality white rum
1 cup ice cubes

Combine all the ingredients in a
cocktail shaker. Shake well and
strain into a chilled cocktail glass.

Bellomonte

Serves 1

1 serving Daiquiri
½ fluid ounce grenadine syrup
½ fluid ounce dark crème de cacao
1 slice lime
1 maraschino cherry, to garnish
1 sprig yerba buena, or other
   fresh mint, to garnish
½ fluid ounce crème de menthe

1 Make a regular Daiquiri and
set aside.

2 Layer the grenadine, crème de cacao,
and lime slice in a highball glass. Pour
the daiquiri on top and garnish with a
maraschino cherry and mint leaves.
Top off with crème de menthe.

Mojito

Serves 1

1 fluid ounce fresh lime juice

6 to 8 leaves fresh yerba buena, or
other fresh mint

⅔ fluid ounce simple syrup, or
2 ounces medium-brown
cane sugar

2 fluid ounces white Habana Club,
or other good quality white rum

1 cup ice cubes

1 fluid ounce lemonade

Dark Habana Club, or other good
quality dark rum

1 sprig yerba buena, or other fresh
mint, to garnish

1 Combine the lime juice, mint leaves, and sugar in a glass.
Crush the mix with a pestle.

2 Add the white rum and fill the glass with ice.

3 Add the lemonade, stir briefly, and top off with the dark rum.

4 Garnish with a sprig of yerba buena and serve with a straw.

Cuba libre

Serves 1

1 cup ice cubes
2 fluid ounces white Habana Club, or
  other good quality white rum
¼ lime (approximately ½ fluid ounce
  fresh lime juice)
Cola

1 Place the ice cubes in a cocktail glass. Add the rum.

2 Squeeze in the lime juice and drop the remaining lime quarter into a glass. Fill with cola and stir.

Banana daiquiri

Serves 1

¾ fluid ounce fresh lime juice
⅔ fluid ounce banana syrup
1 fluid ounce white Habana Club,
  or other good quality white rum
1 fluid ounce dark Habana Club,
  or other good quality dark rum
¼ ripe banana
1 cup crushed ice

Blend all the ingredients in a blender on high speed. Pour into a chilled cocktail glass and serve with a short, thick straw.

Opposite: Cuba libre

Ron Collins

Serves 1

1 fluid ounce fresh lime juice
3 tablespoons sugar
1¾ fluid ounces white rum
1 cup ice cubes
Seltzer
1 slice lime, to garnish
2 maraschino cherries, to garnish

1 Pour the lime juice, sugar, and rum into a Collins glass filled with ice. Top with seltzer and stir briefly.

2 Garnish with a slice of lime and two maraschino cherries. Serve with a straw.

Varadero

Serves 1

¼ fluid ounce lime juice
1 ounce sugar
1 dash bitters
1½ fluid ounces dark Habana Club, or other good quality dark rum
1 cup ice cubes
1 sprig yerba buena, or other fresh mint, to garnish

Pour all the ingredients into an old-fashioned glass, fill with ice, and stir. Garnish with a sprig of mint.

Nacional

Serves 1

¾ fluid ounce pineapple juice
¾ fluid ounce apricot brandy
1½ fluid ounces dark Habana Club, or other good quality dark rum
1 to 2 dashes fresh lime juice
1 cup ice cubes

Mix all the ingredients in a cocktail shaker and strain into a chilled glass.

Above: Mulata

Arenas blancas

Serves 1

1½ fluid ounces white Habana Club,
or other good quality white rum
½ fluid ounce fresh lime juice
½ fluid ounce banana liqueur
½ fluid ounce crème de cacao
½ fluid ounce pineapple juice
1 cup ice cubes
1 wedge of orange, to garnish

Mix all the ingredients except the garnish in a cocktail shaker with ice. Pour into a cocktail glass and garnish with an orange wedge.

Mulata

Serves 1

¾ fluid ounce fresh lime juice
½ fluid ounce simple syrup,
or 1 ounce sugar
¾ fluid ounce brown crème
de cacao
2 fluid ounces dark Habana Club,
or other good quality dark rum
1 fluid ounce maraschino liqueur
1 cup crushed ice
1 slice lime, to garnish

Mix all the ingredients thoroughly on high in a blender and pour into a chilled cocktail glass. Serve with a thick straw and garnish with a slice of lime.

Cuban sidecar

Serves 1

1 fluid ounce fresh lime juice
1 fluid ounce Triple Sec
1 fluid ounce white Habana Club, or
    other good quality white rum
1 cup ice cubes

Mix all the ingredients in a cocktail
shaker and strain into a chilled
cocktail glass dipped in sugar.

Floridita especial

Serves 1

1 fluid ounce red curaçao
1 fluid ounce maraschino liqueur
½ fluid ounce pineapple juice
1 fluid ounce gold rum
Crushed ice

Mix all the ingredients in a cocktail
shaker and pour into a chilled
Champagne flute.

Opposite: Cuban sidecar

Above: Saoco

Saoco

Serves 1

2 fluid ounces white rum
3 fluid ounces sweet coconut milk
½ cup ice cubes

Pour the rum and coconut milk over the ice cubes into a tumbler. Stir and serve with a straw.

Habanero especial

Serves 1

1¾ fluid ounces pineapple juice
1 fluid ounce simple syrup
1 fluid ounce maraschino liqueur
1¾ fluid ounces white rum
1 cup ice cubes
1 maraschino cherry, to garnish

Mix all the ingredients except the garnish in a cocktail shaker and strain into a chilled cocktail glass. Garnish with a maraschino cherry on a stick placed across the rim of the glass.

Above: Papa Hemingway

Cubano especial

Serves 1

½ fluid ounce fresh lime juice

¾ fluid ounce pineapple juice

½ fluid ounce **Triple Sec**

1¾ fluid ounces white **Habana Club**, or
   other good quality white rum

1 cup ice cubes

Mix all the ingredients well in
a cocktail shaker and strain into
a chilled cocktail glass.

Papa Hemingway

Serves 1

¾ fluid ounce fresh lime juice

1¼ fluid ounces fresh grapefruit juice

½ fluid ounce maraschino liqueur

3 fluid ounces white **Habana Club**,
   or other good quality white rum

1 cup crushed ice

Thoroughly blend all the ingredients
in a blender on high and pour into
a chilled tumbler. Serve with a
thick straw.

Above: Presidente

Isla de pinos

Serves 1

1½ fluid ounces grapefruit juice
1 ounce cane sugar
1 fluid ounce grenadine syrup
2 fluid ounces white rum
1 cup ice cubes
½ slice grapefruit, to garnish

1 Mix all the ingredients in a blender and pour into a chilled cocktail glass.

2 Garnish with half a slice of grapefruit wedged on the edge of the glass and serve with a thick straw.

Presidente

Serves 1

1½ fluid ounces white **Habana Club,**
   or other good quality white rum
½ fluid ounce extra dry vermouth
½ fluid ounce sweet vermouth
¼ fluid ounce **Triple Sec**
1 cup ice cubes
Orange wedge
2 maraschino cherries, stems removed,
   to garnish

Stir all the ingredients in a cocktail shaker and strain into a chilled cocktail glass. Squeeze the orange wedge, drop it into the glass, and garnish with two maraschino cherries.

Index

A
Albondigas 97
Arenas blancas 169
Arroz
  amarillo 126
  con gandules 128
  con leche 154
  con pollo 127
  Cubano 136
Asopado de mariscos 122
Avispa 163
Avocado and
  chayote salad 49
  dressing 62

B
Bacalao a la Viscaina 76
Baked Ham 94
Banana daiquiri 166
Beef
  crispy shredded 104
  Cuban hamburger 58
  Cuban meatballs 99
  Cuban-style beef stew
    103
  Cuban-style ground 99
  panseared steak 106
  salt-cured 111
  stewed shredded 102
  sweet plantain and beef
    cakes 130
Bellomonte 164
Bistec a la plancha 106
Bocaditos de bonito 23
Boniato anaranjado 140
Bread pudding, Cuban 141
Buñuelos de boniato
  y yuca 144

C
Cabbage, Spanish
  sausage, and chickpea
  soup 55
Café
  con leche 162
  Cubano 161
  flameado 162
  jengibre 161
Calamares rellenos 74–5
Caldosa 101
Camarones rebozados 80
Candied citrus rind 147
Caramelized milk 146
Caramelized papaya 149
Carne mechada 103
Casserole, fish 73

Chayote and avocado
  salad 49
Cheese
  and guava turnovers
    142
  ham, roasted pork and
    Swiss cheese on sweet
    bread 38
Cherna a la Valenciana 77
Chicharos requetecubanos
  45
Chicken
  caldosa stew 101
  croquettes 18
  Cuban-style chicken-
    flavored rice 127
  Grandmother's chicken
    soup 53
Chickpea, Cabbage, and
  Spanish sausage
  soup 55
Chilindrón de
  cordero 96
Chocolate pudding 152
Choripan 46–7
Chorizo sandwich 46–7
Chuletas de cerdo al estilo
  Cubano 100
Churros 150
Cocido Habanero 55
Cocktail tropical 27
Coconut macaroons 148
Cod, salt
  salad 33
  Viscaya-style 76
Coffee 161–3
Congris oriental 134
Corn
  fritters 25
  pudding 146
  soft corn pudding with
    crabmeat 87
  stew 50
Corn on cob, grilled 121
Crabmeat, soft corn
  pudding with 87
Creole
  salad 54
  sauce 64
  style shrimp 82
Croquetas
  croqueta preparada 32
  de jamón 17
  de mariscos 19
  de pollo 18
  tres croquetas 16

Croquettes 16
  chicken 18
  croquette sandwich 32
  ham 17
  seafood 19
Cuba libre 166
Cuban sidecar 171
Cuban-style Pork Chops 100
Cubano especial 172
Custard 158

D
Daiquiri 164
  banana 166
Dulce
  de cascaras 147
  de leche 146
  de papaya 149

E
Enchilado
  de camarones 82
  de cason 24
Ensalada
  criolla 54
  de bacalao 33
  de chayote y
    aguacate 49
  de coditos 44
  de mariscos 36–7
  real 32
Entremes de camarones 30
Escabeche de bonito 92

F
Fish
  bite-sized tuna
    sandwich snack 23
  casserole 73
  fritters 88
  grouper, Valencia-style
    77
  homemade fish sausage
    70–1
  pickled tuna 92
  roasted red snapper 85
  salt cod salad 33
  salt cod,
    Viscaya-style 76
  skate with caper
    sauce 81
  whole red snapper
    stuffed with
    seafood 78
Flan 158
Floridita especial 171

Fricasé de conejo 109
Frita Cubana 58
Fritters
  corn 25
  Cuban white sweet
    potato and yuca 144
  fish 88
  taro root 120
Fritura de ostiones 28
Frituras
  de maíz 25
  de malanga 120
  de pescado 88
Fufú de plátanos moderno
  121

G
Garlic sauce, hot 68
Grouper, Valencia-style 77
Guava and cheese
  turnovers 142
Guiso de maíz 50
Guiso de quimbobo 43

H
Habanero especial 172
Hallacas vegetarianas 132
Ham
  roasted 94
  with roasted pork and
    Swiss cheese on
    sweet bread 38
  slow-cooked Cuban ham
    with sherry
    vinegar 115
Ham croquettes 17
Hamburger, Cuban 58
Harina con cangrejo 87
Hearts of palm salad 32

I
Isla de pinos 174

J
Judías 48

L
Lamb and roasted pepper
  stew 96
Langosta Criolla 89
Lobster, Cuban-style 89

M
Macaroons, coconut 148
Majarete 146
Mango marmalade 152

Marinade
  basic Cuban 62
  bitter orange 67
  blender 60
Marinado
  Cubano basico 62
  de batidora 60
  de naranja agria 67
Mariquitas 22
Mariscada 34
Marmalade, mango 152
Masitas de cerdo
  fritas 116
Mazorca carboncilla 121
Meatballs, Cuban 99
Media noche 38
Mermelada de
  mango 152
Mojito 165
Mojo criollo para viandas
  y carnes 68
Moros y cristianos 131
Muffins, Cuban-style
  sweet potato 138
Mulata 169

N
Nacional 168
Natilla de chocolate 152–3

O
Octopus, Galician-style 90
Okra stew 43
Oranges
  bitter orange marinade
    67
  orange-scented candied
    sweet potato 140
Oxtail stew 112
Oysters, Cuban-style
  fried 28

P
Pan con lechón 57
Pan de boniato 138
Panatela del trópico 155
Papa Hemingway 173
Papaya, caramelized 149
Pargo asado 85
Pargo relleno 78
Pasta salad,
  Cuban-style 44
Pasteles de guayaba y
  queso 142
Pernil asado 94
Picadillo
  fried green plantains
    topped with 20
  santiaguero 99
Pigeon pea rice 128
Pionono 130

Plantains
  crispy fried plantain
    slices 22
  fried green, topped with
    picadillo 20
  fried sweet and green
    118
  roasted sweet 136
  sweet plantain and beef
    cakes 130
  sweet plantain
    mash 121
Platános en tentación 136
Pork
  Cuban hamburger 58
  Cuban-style pork
    chops 100
  fried pork chunks 116
  ham, roasted pork and
    Swiss cheese on sweet
    bread 38
  sandwich 57
Pound cake, Cuban 155
Presidente 174
Pudín de pan 141
Pudín de pescado 73
Pulpo a la gallega 90
Pulses
  black bean soup 42
  cabbage, Spanish
    sausage, and chickpea
    soup 55
  Cuban-style Split pea
    soup 45
  red bean soup 40
  rice and black
    beans 134
  rice and red beans 131
  white bean soup 48

R
Rabbit fricassee 109
Rabo encendido 112
Raya alcaparrada 81
Red snapper
  roasted 85
  stuffed with seafood 78
Rice
  and black beans 134
  Cuban-style chicken-
    flavored 127
  Cuban-style
    white 136
  pigeon pea 128
  pudding 154
  and red beans 131
  Spanish 126
Rocio de gallo 163
Rolls, sweet 150
Ron Collins 168
Ropa vieja 102

S
Salad
  chayote and avocado 49
  creole 54
  Cuban-style pasta 44
  hearts of palm 32
  salt cod 33
  seafood 36–7
Salpicón de jamón 115
Salpicón de pescado 70–1
Salsa
  Criolla 64
  de aguacate 62
  de tomate Cubana 64–5
Sandwich
  bite-sized tuna
    sandwich snack 23
  chorizo 46–7
  croquette 32
  Cubano 46
  pork 57
Saoco 173
Seafood
  croquettes 19
  Cuban-style lobster 89
  octopus,
    Galician-style 90
  salad 36–7
  soft corn pudding with
    crabmeat 87
  soup 34
  stew 122
  stuffed squid 74–5
  whole red snapper
    stuffed with 78
Shark, creole-style
  baby 24
Shrimp
  creole-style 82
  egg-battered 80
  fresh, with cocktail
    sauce 27
  tapas 30
Skate with caper sauce 81
Sofrito 66
Sopa
  de frijoles colorados 40
  de frijoles negros 42
  de pollo de la abuela 53
Soup
  black bean 42
  cabbage, Spanish
    sausage, and
    chickpea 55
  cold yuca 39
  Cuban-style split pea 45
  Grandmother's
    chicken 53
  red bean 40
  seafood 34
  white bean 48

Split pea soup 45
Squid, stuffed 74–5
Star anise syrup, Cuban
  sweet toast with 157
Stew
  caldosa 101
  corn 50
  Cuban-style beef 103
  lamb and roasted
    pepper 96
  okra 43
  oxtail 112
  seafood 122
Stewed shredded beef 102
Sweet potato
  muffins, Cuban-style 138
  orange-scented
    candied 140
  and yuca fritters 144
Sweet toast with star
  anise syrup 157
Sweetcorn Fritters 25

T
Tamales, vegetarian 132
Tapas, shrimp 30
Taro root fritters 120
Tasajo camagueyano 111
Tomato sauce,
  Cuban-style 64–5
Torrejas 157
Tostones
  con picadillo de cayo
    hueso 20
  y maduros 118
Tres croquetas 16
Tuna
  bite-sized tuna
    sandwich snack 23
  pickled 92
Turnovers, guava and
  cheese 142
Turrón de coco 148

V
Vaca frita 104
Varadero 168
Vegetarian tamales 132
Vinagreta Cubana 60
Vinaigrette, Cuban 60

Y
Yuca
  cold yuca soup 39
  con mojo 125
  crispy yuca sticks 124
  frita 124
  in hot garlic sauce 125
  and sweet potato
    fritters 144
Yucassoise 39